W9-BTA-803

Beijing

（英）Douglas Scott　译

THE SPIRIT OF DISCOVERY

外语教学与研究出版社
FOREIGN LANGUAGE TEACHING AND RESEARCH PRESS

京权图字：01-2008-3661

图书在版编目(CIP)数据

北京=MICHELIN Beijing Guide：英文/法国米其林旅游出版公司编著.—北京：外语教学与研究出版社，2008.8
(米其林旅游指南)
ISBN 978-7-5600-7738-3

Ⅰ. 北… Ⅱ. 法… Ⅲ. 旅游指南—北京市—英文 Ⅳ. K928.91

中国版本图书馆CIP数据核字（2008）第126692号

出 版 人：于春迟
责任编辑：徐　珊
装帧设计：赵　欣
出版发行：外语教学与研究出版社
社　　址：北京市西三环北路19号(100089)
网　　址：http://www.fltrp.com
印　　刷：北京华联印刷有限公司
开　　本：787×1092　1/32
印　　张：7.5
版　　次：2008年8月第1版
　　　　　2008年8月第1次印刷
书　　号：ISBN 978-7-5600-7738-3
定　　价：45.00元
＊　　　　＊　　　　＊
如有印刷、装订质量问题出版社负责调换
制售盗版必究　举报查实奖励
版权保护办公室举报电话：(010)88817519
物料号：177380001

Legal notices for the flyleaf

Collection under the supervision of Florence Dyan

Editors Natacha Brumard, Hervé Deguine

Contributors Gautier Battistella, Geneviève Clastres,
Hervé Deguine, Clélie Dudon,
Françoise Dupont, Serge Guillot,
Victoria Jonathan, Hervé Kerros,
Thierry Sanjuan

Maps Michèle Cana, Dominique Defranchi
Thierry Lemasson, Zhengxin Li
Shandong Provincial Map Publishing House,

Acknowledgements Anaïs Martane, Laurent Fischler,
Léo de Boisgisson, Marie Terrieux

Beijing, the ancient capital city of China, has become an ever-expanding international stage for people from different cultures thanks to the 29th Olympic Games, which kicked off with a grand ceremony in Beijing on August 8, 2008. The Olympic dream, with its universal appeal, can best bridge the differences between tradition and modernity, the West and the East.

Bridging Chinese and other cultures has always been the pursuit of the Foreign Language Teaching and Research Press (FLTRP). And we are not alone in this endeavor. Many people and organizations share our ideal, and Michelin Maps and Guides is one of them.

Our common interest in exploring innovative ways to present China to the outside world has led to our cooperation in developing a series of travel guides to Chinese destinations, with Beijing as the starting point.

The *Michelin Beijing Guide* comprises of three parts: General Practical Information, Discover Beijing, and Walking Tours, encompassing cultural attractions, art highlights, historic sites and relics, transportation and accommodation, shopping and restaurants. Of particular interest to overseas visitors are the eight tailored walking tours of secluded alleys and sights, not necessarily covered by travel agencies.

With Michelin's focus on on-the-spot experience and FLTRP's local resources, the *Michelin Beijing Guide* will assist you in a pleasant tour of this ancient city of modern vitality.

Welcome to Beijing!

Foreign Language Teaching and Research Press

This Beijing guide does not pretend to be exhaustive. It is a practical guide designed for those who travel with limited time and unlimited curiosity. It will help you to focus your attention on the most interesting aspects of the city, whether it is about architecture, society, tradition, modernity, museums, shopping malls, food, nightlife or many other topics. Although very selective, the content of this guide is already much more than what you can expect to do in a week, not to mention a few days. Never mind! Beijing is such an attractive city that, for sure, you will come again and continue your exploration next time.

The guide is divided into key chapters, each of them referring to a specific district of the city. Beijing, as you will quickly realize, is a large city. A very, very large city. It takes time before one really understands what this means. Moving from one side of the city to the other may take more than two or three hours by car on highways… This is why we strongly recommend that you focus on a specific district for a complete visit instead of picking up points of interest on the map and wasting a lot of time jumping from one part of the city to another.

We have tried our best to put the most up-to-date information in the following pages. However, Beijing is a restless city. What was true last month may not be true today. Please, accept our apology in advance for the inconveniency such rapid change may cause you. And always try to give a call to where you plan to go before you start moving.

One more point: please do not hesitate to ask for help from Beijing people. Most of the citizens may not be able to communicate with you in English, but all of them will do their best to find an English speaker and help you to find your way. This is the tradition of hospitality of Beijing.

We wish you a nice stay in Beijing!

The Michelin Beijing Team

General practical information | 1

Preparing for the trip   2

Local time   2
How to make calls in China   2
When to go   2
Making reservations   2
Formalities   3
Health   4
Money   5
Things to take with you   6
Travel for all   6

A to Z listing   7

Bank /Exchange   7
Cigarettes   7
Electricity   8
Embassies in Beijing   8
Health   9
Holidays   9
Internet   10
Laundry   10
Mail   10
Media   10
Museums, monuments and
  tourist sites   11
Opening time   13
Photography   13
Public toilets   14
Security   14
Tap water   14
Telephone   14
Tipping   15
Tourism offices   16
Units of length   16
Weather   16

Etiquette   16

Chinese manners   17
Eating at the restaurant with
  Chinese people   17
Must dos   17
Don't dos   18

Accommodation   19

Prices   19
Where to stay   19

Eating out   20

The menu   21
Prices   21
Where to eat   21
Chinese food   22
Some useful words in restaurant   24

Entertainment   26

Sporting and activities   26
Cultural life   26
Night life   27
Holidays, festivals and events   29

Shopping   30

Bargaining   30
Arts and crafts   30
Other purchases   31
Where to shop   33
Sending your purchases home   33

Getting by in Chinese   33

Pinyin   33
Holding a conversation   35
Getting around, visiting   36
Daily life   37
The family   38
Transport   39
Numbers   39
Colours   40
Time   41
At the restaurant   41
At the hotel   42
At the market   43
At the bank   43
At the hospital   43

Discover Beijing | 45

Getting to Beijing   46

By air   46
By train   48
By bus   49

Getting around   49

2008: Beijing Olympics   56

Olympic Sports Venues (in Beijing)   58

How to get about   60

Useful addresses   61

Tourism office   61
Banks/Exchanges   62
Post office   62
Telephone   62
Internet   62
Emergencies/Health   63

Where to stay   63

Around the Forbidden City and
   Wangfujing   64

Around Deshengmen   67

Sanlitun and Chaoyang District   70

Around Dongzhimen   72

South of Qianmen   73

Where to eat   74

Around the Forbidden City and
   Wangfujing   74
Around Deshengmen   76
Sanlitun and Chaoyang District   79
Around Dongzhimen   80
South of Qianmen   81
In the west of the city   82

Going out for a drink   82

In the Lake Area   83
In Sanlitun   84
In Chaoyang District   85

Things to do   87

Guied Tours of Beijing   87
Sporting activities   87
Cinema   88
Massage   88
Shows   89
Popular shows   91
Shopping   91
Beijing art   102

History   106

Walking tours | 117

1 **The Forbidden City and Wangfujing**   118

2 **Around Deshengmen**   140

3 **Sanlitun and Chaoyang District**   150

4 **Around Dongzhimen**   157

5 **South of Qianmen**   163

6 **West Beijing**   175

7 **Around Beijing**   189

8 **The Great Wall and the Imperial Tombs**   195

Preparing for the trip   2

A to Z listing   7

Etiquette   16

Accommodation   19

Eating out   20

Entertainment   26

Shopping   30

Getting by in Chinese   33

GENERAL PRACTICAL INFORMATION

Preparing for the trip

Local time

In China, the official time is GMT +8; when it is noon in Beijing in summer, it is 6am in Paris (same day), 5am in London (same day), 12am in Washington (day before), and 2pm in Sydney (same day).

How to make calls in China

The International code for China is 86. The code for Beijing is 10. So, to call Beijing from Paris, you need to dial 00 86 10 followed by the eight digit number.

When to go

Beijing has a continental climate: spring and autumn are the best seasons. During these intermediate seasons, which are quite short (about two months each), temperatures are mild and rainfall relatively low. In spring you can admire everywhere the first blossoms of the year (April—May). In autumn, trees take on magnificent red colours (September—October). Warning: in May a sandy wind can blow up from the Gobi Desert and sweep over the Beijing region. From June to September, summer is a byword for heat and humidity over many regions of China, with an often hazy sky and smog covering major areas of the city of Beijing. In winter (November—March) the climate is a bit harsh (-15°C to -2 °C), but it's dry cold, with clear blue skies. Finally you should be aware that it's cheaper to travel in winter: tourists are fewer and the majority of hotels drop their prices.

It is not recommended to go during the two Chinese holidays: one week between mid January and mid February (corresponding to Chinese New Year), and the first week of October (National Day). These two weeks are the "Golden Weeks". Chinese tourists are very large in number then and prices can vary up to four times the norm.

Making reservations

The high seasons are the two "Golden Weeks" (see above). It is then almost impossible to get a train or flight ticket, or even a hotel with

rooms. Warning: during the four days which follow the Chinese New Year, almost all activities cease. (A few public transport and a few restaurants are open.)

Formalities

This is for information only. It is recommended that foreign visitors contact the Chinese Embassy or Consulate in their own country for more recent details at the time of their visit.

Travellers from the EU, as well as Canada, must be in possession of a visa, issued by the Chinese Consulate, and a passport valid for at least six months after the date of departure from Chinese territory.

The tourist visa is valid for thirty days or 3 months from the date of issue.

The tourist visa can generally be extended for 30 days, handled by the Exit and Entry Management Section, Beijing Municipal Public Security Bureau [address: No.2, Andingmen Dongdajie, Dongcheng District, Beijing, Tel (010)84020101].

The visa does not cover entry to Tibet; this autonomous region is subject to a special permit.

▶ *Vaccinations*

No vaccination is compulsory. It is however recommended to

vaccinate against tetanus and polio. It is also advised to be vaccinated against diphtheria, typhoid, hepatitis A and B and meningitis.

▶ Driving licence

To drive in China, you must have a Chinese driving licence. International Driving Permits are not recognised.

Health

▶ Illnesses

Intestinal problems caused by a change of diet occur frequently. Moreover, food is often a little spicy in China. Wash fruit and vegetables well as the risk of amoebiasis (dysentery) is high.

As for avian flu, the Department of Health recommends traveller avoid all contact with poultry and birds: not to go to poultry farms or bird markets; avoid eating any food products that are raw or under-cooked, particularly meat and eggs, and wash your hands often in soap and water. Equally, you should avoid drinking tap water.

▶ Medicine kit

Put together a small first aid kit to include the main necessities: aspirin or paracetamol, anti-diarrhoea tablets (such as Imodium), suntan cream, elastoplast, antiseptic lotion for minor injuries and mosquito spray.

▶ Medical services

First Aid—Peking Union offers a medical centre capable of supporting the best care. In case of any serious problems, arrange repatriation (see the section "Insurance").

Do not hesitate to contact hotel reception or that of a major hotel to be understood by the doctor.

Hospitals—Peking University Medical College Hospital, in Beijing. Tel (010)65295153.

Do not hesitate to contact the panel doctor of your Embassy or the nearest Consulate (see the section "Useful addresses").

Pharmacies—Bring your usual medicines, but be aware that excellent medicines are available locally; the Chinese pharmacopoeia based on herbs offers effective remedies. Most chemists have available both western medicines and traditional medicine products.

Doctors—There are doctors of both traditional Chinese medicine and western medicine in hospitals. With a single call, the Consulate can give you a list of doctors regularly used by expats.

In any emergency dial 120.

▶ Insurance

Check with your insurer that you are covered abroad, and in China in particular. If you travel with a tour operator, check that insurance assistance/repatriation is included in the cost of your holiday.

Money

▶ Currency

The monetary unit is Renminbi (literally "people's money") or yuan (CNY, RMB or ¥), divided into 10 *jiao*. Its exchange rate is linked to a basket of currencies based mainly on the USD, the EUR, CHF and so on. In July 2008, 1 Euro was equivalent to 10.770 yuan. The Chinese do not often use the term "*yuan*"(元) in ordinary

	RMB
EUR 1	10.770
USD 1	6.849
AUD 1	6.566
GBP 1	13.563
CHF 1	6.654

Note: data obtained in July 10th, 2008

speech: they'd rather use "*kuai*" (块 , literally "monetary unit"); in the same way they talk of "*mao*"(毛) to indicate "*jiao*" (角 , literally "one tenth of a unit").

▶ Exchange

You can only change Chinese currency in China, but it is now possible to buy yuan outside the country in small quantities: check with your bank or at a bureau of change to find out if they have any in stock. In China you can exchange your foreign currency in bank branches, at airports or in hotels (where the rate of tax is higher). To find out the rate, check the website www.xe.com.

When you buy yuan, look after the receipt: it will allow you eventually to change back the remaining yuan when you leave, up to half of the initial sum exchanged. Have your passport with you.

▶ Travellers cheques

Very useful to prevent theft, travellers cheques in foreign currencies can be converted into yuan at all Exchanges (look for the sign "Change"). American Express travellers cheques let you claim a refund within 24 hours in case of theft and do not have an expiry date.

Don't forget to sign your cheques once you receive them.

▶ Credit cards

Automatic cash machines, indicated in China by "ATM" (for Automatic Teller Machine), are widespread, but don't necessarily accept all foreign credit cards: check the name of your card. Visa, Premier, Cirrus, PLUS or Maestro are generally the most accepted. A large proportion of hotels and restaurants accept equally payments by card. Consider asking your provider for the number to call from abroad to report lost or stolen cards.

Cash withdrawal is much more attractive from an ATM than at the counter: the commission rate fixed by your bank is often less (check with your customer advisor).

Things to take with you

▶ Clothes

In summer, reckon on light clothes (cotton rather than synthetic), and in spring and autumn take a few warm clothes as well as seasonal outfits. In winter you'd better take woollen jumpers, gloves, hat, windbreaker and warm socks.

There are no particular dress codes for visiting religious places, a large amount of tolerance being exercised. Nevertheless, avoid extravagant behaviour and respect silence.

▶ Making gifts locally

In no matter what situation, Chinese will not hesitate to help, and always with a smile. So think about taking with you a few small items from your country. They will know how to show appreciation for the gesture, even if they may refuse first time, as is the general rule in China.

Travel for all

▶ Travelling with children

Every hotel will agree, for a small cost, to offer an extra bed in your room for a child.

▶ Women travelling on their own

They can travel peacefully and are not even bothered in the street. Women should only avoid going out alone in the middle of the night.

▶ Travelling as a couple

Chinese couples are generally very modest in public, even if today this is changing in large towns. They however don't mind foreigners, as long as the latter know how to limit their amorous enthusiasm!

▶ *Senior travellers*

The Chinese do not hesitate to give up their seat on public transports. Underground stations are equipped with escalators (at least to go up). Shopping centres and almost all hotels have lifts.

▶ *Disabled travellers*

There are lifts in almost all buildings and there are many low level pavements (at the access points of underpasses or bridges). Public toilets, major hotels and museums are gradually becoming equipped with disabled facilities.

▶ *Travelling with pets*

It is impossible to travel together with a pet: you need to present to customs an international health certificate issued only 24 hours before departure and an up-to-date vaccination certificate (principally against rabies); in addition, the animals are subject to a 30 day quarantine period on arrival, with compulsory isolation for non-resident pets.

A to Z Listing

Bank/Exchange

The banking network of China is more and more efficient. The large conurbations and small towns popular with tourists are very well provided with bank branches and ATMs accept almost all foreign cards. In the large towns and tourism regions, most banks can exchange foreign currency.

Elsewhere, go and see Bank of China; likewise you can only draw money on a foreign bank account from the counter of a branch of Bank of China.

Cigarettes

China is the world's number 1 manufacturer with almost 2 billion units made each year (35% of global production). You can find a large choice of brands at low prices and tobacconists on every street corner. The law, till now, is becoming stricter. For example, Beijing Municipality has implemented several provisions to ban smoking in most public places starting from May 1, 2008, such as schools, sports arenas, restaurants, bars, Internet cafés and all indoor areas of medical facilities.

Electricity

The current is 220V 50HZ in China, and in the large majority of hotels sockets are adaptable for all systems. Take an adaptor with you to prepare for the unexpected.

Embassies in Beijing

Australian Embassy—21, Dongzhimenwai Dajie, Sanlitun. Tel (010)51404111, www.china.embassy.gov.au

Austrian Embassy—5, Xiushui Nanjie, Jianguomenwai. Tel (010)65322061, www.bmeia.gv.at

Embassy of Kingdom of Belgium—6, Sanlitun Lu, Chaoyang District, Tel (010)65321736, www.diplomatie.be/beijingfr

British Embassy—11, Guanghua Lu, Jianguomenwai. Tel (010)51924000,

www.uk.cn

Canadian Embassy—19, Dongzhimenwai Dajie, Chaoyang District. Tel (010) 65323536, www.beijing.gc.ca.

The Royal Danish Embassy—1, Dongwu Jie, Sanlitun. Tel (010)85329900, www.ambbeijing.um.dk

Embassy of Finland—Level 26, South Tower of Beijing Kerry Centre, No. 1 Guanghua Lu. Tel (010) 85198300, www.finland.cn

French Embassy—3, Dongsan Jie, Sanlitun, Chaoyang District. Tel (010)85328080, www.ambafrance-cn.org.

Embassy of Germany—17, Dongzhimenwai Daijie, Sanlitun. Tel (010)85329000, www.peking.diplo.de

Holland Embassy—4, Liangmahe Nanlu. Tel (010)85320200, www.hollandinchina.org

Embassy of Israel—17, Tianze Lu, Chaoyang District. Tel (010)85320500, http://beijing.mfa.gov.il

Embassy of Italy—2, Dong'er Jie, Sanlitun. Tel (010)85327600, www.ambpechino.esteri.it

Embassy of Japan—7, Ritan Lu, Jianguomenwai. Tel (010)65322361,

www.cn.emb-japan.go.jp

Embassy of the Republic of Korea—20, Dongfang Donglu, Chaoyang District.

Tel (010) 85310700, http://china.koreanembassy.cn

Embassy of Mexico—5, Dongwu Jie, Sanlitun. Tel (010)65322574,

The Royal Norwegian Embassy—1, Dongyi Jie, Sanlitun. Tel (010) 65322261, www.norway.org.cn

Embassy of the Russian Federation—4, Beizhong Jie, Dongzhimennei. Tel (010)65321381, www.russia.org.cn

Singapore Embassy—1, Xiushui Beijie, Jianguomenwai. Tel (010) 65321115, www.mfa.gov.sg

Embassy of Spain—9, Sanlitun Lu Chaoyang District. Tel (010)65321986, www.mae.es/embajadas/pekin

Embassy of Sweden—3, Dongzhimenwai Dajie. Tel (010)65329790, www.swedenabroad.com

Swiss Embassy—3, Dongwu Jie, Sanlitun. Tel (010)85328888, www.eda.admin.ch/beijing

Embassy of the United States—3, Xiushui, Beijie, Jianguomenwai. Tel (010)65323831, http://beijing.usembassy-china.org.cn

Health

Emergency number: Tel 120.

Holidays

1st January: the first day of the year is becoming celebrated more and more in large towns. A day of paid leave.

Chinese New Year (Spring Festival): Chinese New Year (occurring between 20th January and 20th February) begins for the Chinese the first paid week of the year.

Events every day for two weeks, right up to Lantern Festival.

8th March: International Women' Day. A half day of paid leave for all women.

1st May: Labour Day. A day of paid leave for all Chinese working people.

1st October: National Day in memory of the proclamation of the People's Republic of China in 1949. The second week of paid leave for the Chinese.

Each time it's the government who decides precisely which are the 7 days of paid leave. Frequently the weekend preceding is worked.

Internet

Internet cafés with fast ADSL connection are now part of the landscape of large towns in China. Moreover, the countryside is also astonishingly well served by a network of Internet cafés, which are found in even the most far-flung place. The most difficult part is finding them. For that you need to ask a young person where the nearest *Wangba* is: if he's nice he'll take you there so you don't get lost in the maze of aisles in a shop or at the end of an alleyway. Every major hotel offers a "Business Centre" with Internet access, and more and more systematically offer connection points in the rooms. But in a hotel connection costs more than in a *Wangba*. Numerous companies also offer Internet access through a telephone socket.

Laundry

Most hotels offer their guests a laundry service. If your hotel does not have a laundry service, go to the nearest hotel or major residential complex that does: you will certainly get your things washed. You can also find cheap local dry cleaners.

Mail

The Chinese postal service, indicated by the green geometric symbol and neon sign "China Post", is present in every locality, or almost. The offices are open theoretically every day. A large choice of stamps and the Chinese are passionate philatelists. To fix stamps to letters, a pot of glue and a brush are at your disposal. You can also buy stamps in most hotels. Letter boxes can be found everywhere in major towns. Beijing International Post and Telecommunications Office provides a variety of postal services.[address: NO.18, Futong Dongdajie, Wangjing, Chaoyang District, Tel (010)64751689] An Express Mail service (EMS) operates to most countries and to most destinations within China. (address: NO.17, Zhushikou Dongdajie, Chongwen District, service hotline: 11185, www.ems.com.cn/english-main.jsp)

Media

▶ *International newspapers*

The major daily international papers are available in Wangfujing Foreign Laguages Bookstore in Beijing. The big hotels offer guests some English language newspapers.

10

▶ *Chinese newspapers in English*

This has become more developed in the last few years. For sale in kiosks, on the main thoroughfares and in big hotels. You can also easily find *China Daily* in all tourist areas; a Chinese daily with local and international stories.

Some finance magazines are starting to appear as well.

▶ *Free magazines*

That's Beijing, City Weekend, Beijing Talk, Quo..., available in bars, at the entrance of some art galleries, in English or bilingual English/Chinese, devoted to all the news about going out, exhibitions, film times at cinemas, etc.

▶ *Press*

There are more than 500 publishing houses in China. The Foreign Language Teaching and Research Press (FLTRP) is one of the leading foreign language publisher and a rising Chinese language publisher. As an academic and educational publishing house, FLTRP is dedicated to "recording human civilization and bridging world cultures".(www.fltrp.com/en/default.asp)

▶ *Radio*

In mainland China you can receive almost all international radio stations.

▶ *Television*

State television transmits a dozen channels throughout China, to which can be added numerous local and national channels. Major hotels generally receive a whole load of international channels such as TV5 and BBC.

CCTV9 transmits all its programmes in English. Chinese language lessons are also shown.

Museums, monuments and tourist sites

▶ *Times*

Museums are generally open every day, without a break from 9am to 5pm. Temples and parks often open their doors earlier, at between 6am and 8:30am. Admission is permitted up to 30 minutes prior to closing, except the larger museums which bring forward the last admissions to 1 hour before closure.

FLTRP

Recording Human Civilization and Bridging Different Cultures

记载人类文明　沟通世界文化

▶ Prices

The cost of entry varies greatly from one site to another. The margin is in general somewhere between 10 to 60 yuan, but entry to the main natural sites, the most famous monuments and certain popular tourist resorts can cost 100 yuan. In general there is a 50% reduction for children and students, and is free for those under 1.2m.

Opening time

▶ Government offices

Chinese government offices are generally open Monday to Friday from 8:30am to 5:30pm.

▶ Banks

Bank counters in China open generally from 9am to 5pm daily.

▶ Post offices

Post Office branches in China are generally open every day from 9am to 5pm. Some town centre offices close later at 8pm.

▶ Shops

Shops are most often open every day from 9am to 9pm, including holidays. On main roads and in shopping centres, shops and supermarkets prolong their hours of opening until 10pm.

▶ Markets

Vegetable, bird, fish, plant markets... Markets, of which there are very many in China, are generally open every day from 7am to 6pm.

▶ Restaurants

Chinese restaurants are open all day from 10am to 8pm or 9pm. Warning: Outside the large towns, restaurants often close before 8pm as Chinese people eat around 6pm. In Beijing, restaurants often stay open until 9.30pm or 10pm at least, some open even all night. If you get hungry during the night, you can always find a walking food seller on a square in the town centre or local mini-market.

▶ Mini-markets/Drugstores

Open 24/7, they have become more and more numerous, above all in large towns.

Photography

Most people use digital cameras to take photos at tourist sites.

Colour film is very easy to find (supermarkets, kiosks) in tourist areas (100, 200 and 400 ISO). On the other hand slide and black and white film is rarer. We would advise stocking up on these before you go, especially if you are going to the countryside. You can get films developed in a record time and for a very low price in a large number of photo shops close to tourist sites (they even offer other services: scanner, CD of digital photos, etc.). In front of symbolic sites, numerous professional photographers armed with SLR or Polaroid cameras propose taking your photograph for a modest fee. The Chinese are quite easy to accept having their photographs taken, but ask their permission first. In addition they will willingly ask to have a photograph taken with a Westerner: return the favour with your camera!

Public toilets

In China there are free public toilets in towns, identified by signs. In the larger towns you can nevertheless find paying public toilets, regularly cleaned and responding to western standards of comfort. Please take some toilet paper with you.

Security

China is universally safe and violence-free. If pick pocketing does happen sometimes, it's always without violence.

You can contact Beijing Municipal Public Security Bureau in an emergence (Tel 110).

Tap water

Water from the tap is not drinkable. Choose mineral water instead, cheap and easy to find in all local food stores or on the street. Make sure the bottles are tightly sealed.

Telephone

▶ *Fixed line telephones and phone booths*

The Chinese telephone network is well developed and works fairly well. In town there are many phone booths and they accept nearly every phone card: moreover elsewhere, there is always a store which offers the use of a telephone to customers. In hotels, all rooms are equipped with telephone lines, but not all allow overseas calls (access is surcharged: ask at reception), often they are simply internal lines.

▶ *Mobile phones*

In China, mobile telephone numbers begin with 13 or 15 and have 11 digits. You can buy a GSM SIM card from any customer service center of China Mobile (www.chinamobile.com/en/) or China Unicom (www.chinaunicom.com.cn/services/)

▶ *Telephone cards and mobile phone top-ups*

All food stores and mini-markets sell phone cards, usually in units of 50 and 100 yuan. Mobile phone top-up cards cost 50 to 100 yuan. To activate your top-up ask the seller, in exchange for 1 or 2 yuan, to call the operator.

▶ *Local calls*

If you are calling a landline in the same town or on the outskirts, you do not need to dial the local code. If you call another region or province you must dial the code preceded by a certain number, for example 0 or 9.

▶ *International calls*

To call overseas you must dial 00 followed by the country code and the number of the person you are calling.

Telephone cards for calling overseas from a landline—IP Card—are on sale at kiosks and local food stores at the official rate of 100 yuan for 30 to 45 minutes talk time, but you can get them for 50-70 yuan if you bargain.

▶ *Useful numbers*

Emergency: Tel 120.

Police: Tel 110.

Fire: Tel 119.

Directory enquiries: Tel 114.

Weather forecast: Tel 12121 (in English).

Tipping

Tipping does not form part of the habits of the Chinese. Today, it is willingly accepted, above all in Beijing and it is normal now to give a tip in the major hotels. All the same, it's not necessary to leave it in taxis or bars.

Tourism offices

The concept of tourism offices is still new in China. Most towns only have travel agencies like CITS, the national agency which sometimes acts as a tourist information office and whose staff are generally competent. Beijing benefits from a good network of tourist information centres, shown by an "I".

The national tourism department, whose subsidiary, the national tourism office (CNTO), has offices overseas, has only an administration office in Beijing: China National Tourism Administration (CNTA)—Area 9 Jianguomennei Dajie, Chaoyang District, Beijing, Tel (010) 65275315, http://en.cnta.gov.cn/lyen/index.asp.

You can find on the website the country's main attractions and practical information listed by destination.

Beijing Tourism Information Centre—28, Jianguomenwai Dajie, Chaoyang District, Tel (010) 85157056, www.english.bjta.gov.cn. Twenty or so offices situated close to major tourist sites.

Units of length

The metric system is more and more in use to the detriment of the Chinese system, even if the population still very regularly use traditional weight units, notably the *jin* which is equivalent to 500 grams, and units of area, like the *mu* which represents 1/15 of a hectare.

Weather

Weather forecasts are shown on every TV channel and printed in every daily newspaper. You can get forecasts for the next 10 days on the following websites:

www.cma.gov.cn/english/—The website of China Meteorological Administration. In Chinese and English.

Etiquette

The Chinese are very obliging and never hesitate to help in whatever way they can. Naturally extrovert they smile very spontaneously and are very curious about foreigners: outside the large towns expect to be stared at without any malice. You will even often get approached, asked where you come from, how much you earn and if they can have a photo taken with you. To get close to the locals, there's nothing better than addressing them in a few words of Chinese or better still some words in local dialect: they will react enthusiastically!

Chinese manners

The Chinese are masters in the art of social convention and ready made system of manners. For example, it's normal to refuse a gift the first time or to shake the head in response to a simple thank you; and it is completely natural to respond with repeated thanks and compliments. The Chinese do not use the same system of manners as we do. So, saying "hello"," thank you" or "excuse me" is much less widespread than certain down-to-earth questions like "Have you eaten?", "How's the family?", or "Where are you going?".

Eating at the restaurants with Chinese people

It is at the dining table where Chinese manners are the most elaborate. You must show your enthusiasm the whole length of the meal and follow the frantic rhythm of the toasts, begun by the head of the table, by drinking at least a mouthful of your wine; the Chinese will appreciate it if you also offer a toast in their honour. The head of the table, always seated opposite the entrance, will insist also that you have a second helping of the dish or dishes that remain: make them happy at least once or twice. And don't forget that a very dirty table at the end of a meal is a sign that you have had a good evening. Each time when your glass is empty, the head of the table will systematically fill it. Take small mouthfuls of drink.

Must dos

— Shake hands when you greet some, men or women.
— Thank the waiter or waitress when they are serving you by tapping discretely on the table with your index finger.
— Offer small gifts to your Chinese friends when you come back from a trip.
— Give fruits but not flowers when invited to dinner.
— Call an acquaintance by their first name: the forename is reserved for friends.

For others, men or women, you should use the full name or family name (first syllable of the whole name), followed by the person's title. For example, *Wang laoshi*: Teacher Wang; *Lu shifu*: Master Lu.

Don't dos

— Openly criticise the Chinese regime. The Chinese will willingly talk about the changes which have taken place in China in the past years, but avoid criticising the local system.

— Give yourself airs: legendary Chinese modesty prevents one from asserting anything whatsoever on one's own account.

— Direct the spout of the teapot towards someone, particularly around a table: that can bring misfortune to whoever it is pointed at.

— Arrive late for a meeting: the Chinese are always punctual and expect others to be the same.

— Show feelings in public: The Chinese are very modest and do not generally let their feelings be shown in front of others.

— Share a bill. An invitation expects another in return: it's the best way of showing that you like someone.

— Make a Chinese host open the gift you made in front of you: he'll open it after you've gone.

Accommodation

Chinese hotel infrastructure has considerably become developed over the past ten years or so. Every town now has on offer accommodation for every comfort level and the great majority of establishments offer a range of standard equipments (telephone, television, etc.).

Keep your hotel's business card with its name in Chinese: you can show it to a taxi driver so that he can drive you back.

Prices

Our selection is classified by price, on the basis of a double room in high season with breakfast included. In certain cases, the price of breakfast is shown separately and if the establishment doesn't offer breakfast, we'll show it in the text. Out of season, the price of rooms systematically becomes subject to reduction from 20% to 60% in relation to the summer rate, except luxury hotels. Note also that accommodation is payable in advance.

Where to stay

▶ *Youth hostels*

Youth hostels marked "Hostelling International" are more and more common, you'll find several in Beijing. They are usually well looked after, with English speaking staff and offer almost always doubles, in addition to dormitories. On the other hand they aren't necessarily any cheaper than the cheapest local hotels. If you don't have the international member card (Hostelling International Card), you can always buy one at the youth hostel counter or pay a little more.

www.hihostels.com—On this website you can book your room or bed. Reservation is recommended all year round, the number of youth hostels being still few compared with the level of demand.

www.yhachina.com—This website keeps a register of Hostelling International members in the majority of Chinese towns. Reservation available online.

▶ *Guesthouses*

They are almost all situated outside of towns, in villages or near natural tourist sites. The rooms are usually very modest, but offer what you need. The bathrooms are shared and the toilets are often no more than a simple ditch. It's always possible to eat something there, and with a small financial contribution, the mistress of the house will go out of her way to prepare a meal for you.

▶ *Hotels*

Hotels represent the near total of the available accommodation in China. They are classed from 1 to 5 stars. The majority belong to international hotel chains; national consortiums run by overseas Chinese, where there is a certain level of standards but compensate for it with a somewhat general level of comfort: private bathrooms, TV, telephone (which sometimes only allows you to call reception), air conditioning, etc. The establishments are generally well maintained depending on the category, but you will come across certain hotels with old bathrooms and worn carpets. Different rates are applied to double bedrooms (a double bed) and those with two beds, the latter being more expensive. The prices given at reception are systematically reduced out of season. On the internet websites of the big international and Chinese chains you'll find exclusive deals and can book online:

www1.hilton.com—Attractive deals at Hilton hotels in major Chinese cities.

www.jinjianghotels.com—The website of the Jin Jiang Hotels.

www.shangri-la.com—The website of the luxury Shangri-La hotel group.

Eating out

There is an air of conviviality around the Chinese dining table. A certain number of dishes are ordered which are placed at the centre of the table and which each guest picks at with their chopsticks. At banquets the Chinese calculate one dish per guest, in a restaurant count two dishes for one person dining alone and three dishes for two people. In Beijing, however many restaurants follow the western principal of one dish per person. In tourist areas, most establishments have knives and forks. Elsewhere on the other hand it's impossible to avoid chopsticks.

The Chinese eat relatively early compared with us: breakfast is before 8am, lunch 11am to 1pm and dinner around 6:30pm.

The menu

Choice is one quality you expect of a restaurant in China. The menu therefore is long, classified by the types of dishes. The majority of restaurants in town and at tourist sites now offer menus translated into English and/or accompanied by photos of the main dishes. In the countryside, ordering is done more often in the kitchen where you are shown directly the vegetables and meat in the fridge. When there is neither a translation nor photos, the best thing to do is to have a look at the other tables: the customers will know how to make themselves understood.

Prices

The Chinese love going out to eat. Restaurants are therefore plentiful and in the main cheap. Reckon on 50 yuan per head to satisfy your appetite in a traditional restaurant. Gourmet restaurants offering food influenced by international tastes will have much the same prices as those in France (200-300 yuan/person).

Warning: If you order fish, the price depends on the weight.

Where to eat

▶ *In hotels, guesthouses and youth hostels*

The majority of hotels serve meals throughout the day (usually from 7am) for the three daily meals. You can even eat there if you are a non-resident. The biggest establishments offer quality food, but their rates are often greater than similarly rated restaurants. In other types of establishments, the prices are sensibly the same as in restaurants. It is possible to order a snack any time of the day in the majority of youth hostels.

▶ *In restaurants*

With the exception of numerous foreign and fusion restaurants patronised by Westerners, the restaurants in Beijing serve Chinese food which often marries local gourmet food with well-known international dishes. Certain local chains, particularly those run by Chinese are specialised, for example in Mongolian hotpot or dim-sum, Cantonese style dumplings with a thousand varieties. You can also find a growing number of bars and switched-on cafés which mix classic Chinese food with international dishes found anywhere: pizzas, hamburgers, spaghetti, etc. In the small, busy and numerous popular restaurants, you can prepare your soup by choosing the ingredients yourself and savour in all simplicity pancakes, doughnuts, stuffed breads, dumplings, fried noodles, kebabs, etc.

Chinese food

Warning: With the exception of Shanghai regional specialities, which are rather sweet and sour, some Chinese food is spicy, maybe too spicy in Hunan and Sichuan.

Those who cannot stand this type of food should use the phrase *bú là de*, which means "not spicy".

A typical Chinese meal starts with cold dishes known as "small dishes", continues with hot food, called "main dishes", and ends with a soup which can then on rare occasions go on to a dessert.

▶ *Specialities*

You can find below some of the most currently used ingredients in cooking and some of the well-known specialities:

Fried Beef in Ginger (gānbiān niúròu, 干煸牛肉): northern Chinese speciality.

Beijing Duck (běijīng kǎoyā, 北京烤鸭): that is to say coated in melted sugar, then roasted and served hot or cold.

Chinese cabbage (báicài, 白菜): usually stir-fried, it is one of the most used vegetables in Chinese cooking.

New Year Rice Cake (niángāo, 年糕): made from glutinous rice flour, sugar, lard and water.

Preserved eggs (sōnghuādàn, 松花蛋): duck eggs preserved for 3 months in a mixture of straw, clay and quicklime, so called because of the dark and veined surface. Very popular, they symbolise longevity and boldness.

Noodles (miàntiáo, 面条): Chinese noodles have been around for 2,000 years and are prepared with various ingredients: wheat (miàn), the most used, but also rice (mǐfěn; in this case they are called rice noodles), or even bean, lentil, etc. You can have the famous beef noodle, made on the spot, but also noodles fried in a wok with meat.

Steamed Stuffed Buns (bāozi, 包子): enjoyed at any time of the day by the Chinese, these buns, which come in various forms according to the region and the makers, are steamed and stuffed or not with a filling made from meat and/or vegetables.

Sweet-Sour Crucian (tángcù jìyú, 糖醋鲫鱼): freshwater fish with firm and tasty meat, fried then covered in a sweet red sauce.

Kung Pao Chicken (gōngbǎo jīdīng, 宫保鸡丁): a particularly highly seasoned speciality, originally from Sichuan.

Sharks Fin Soup (yúchìtāng, 鱼翅汤): a great Cantonese speciality.

Stuffed Dumplings (jiǎozi, 饺子): half-moon shaped dumplings, consisting of a pastry made from flour and filled with minced meat (pork, beef, lamb) and vegetables fragranced with garlic, onion, or ginger. And as the Chinese saying goes: "Nothing is more comfortable than having a lie-down; nothing is more delicious than stuffed dumpling!"

Tofu (dòufu, 豆腐): a product made from soy beans soaked then reduced to a purée which is then boiled, filtered and turned to gel. Very rich in vegetable proteins and easily digested, it is often served in cubes or in strips.

▶ *Some useful words in restaurants:*

English	Pinyin	Chinese characters
Tea	chá	茶
Coffee	kāfēi	咖啡
Milk	niúnǎi	牛奶
Mineral water	kuàngquánshuǐ	矿泉水
Boiled water	kāishuǐ	开水
White wine	báipútaojiǔ	白葡萄酒
Red wine	hóngpútaojiǔ	红葡萄酒
Rice wine	mǐjiǔ	米酒
Beer	píjiǔ	啤酒
Roast Duck	kǎoyā	烤鸭
Chinese cabbage	báicài	白菜
Preserved eggs	sōnghuādàn	松花蛋
Noodles	miàntiáo	面条
Steamed buns	miànbāo	面包
Fish	yúròu	鱼肉
Kung Pao Chicken	gōngbǎo jīdīng	宫保鸡丁
Bamboo shoots	zhúsǔn	竹笋
Stuffed Dumplings	jiǎozi	饺子
Rice	mǐfàn	米饭
Soup	tāng	汤
Tofu	dòufu	豆腐
Beef	niúròu	牛肉
Pork	zhūròu	猪肉

Lamb	yángròu	羊肉
Snake	shéròu	蛇肉
Bill/Check	mǎidān/jiézhàng	买单／结账
Chopsticks	kuàizi	筷子
Knife/fork	dāozi/chǎzi	刀子／叉子
Menu	càidān	菜单
Not spicy	bú là de	不辣的
Spicy	là de	辣的

▶ Drinks

Tea is the most common and most consumed drink in China. In a restaurant, you are served it as soon as you arrive, but it is not a drink to have with the meal: the Chinese prefer a beer or alcohol with their food.

The largest consumer of beer since 2004, China makes almost all the brands on sale itself. Apart from the well-known Tsingtao and Yanjing, products of the town of the same name Qingdao and Beijing, each region makes its own beer.

Traditional Chinese alcohols are determined by the colour with which they are associated: yellow wines are rice wines having the same alcohol content as our grape wine. The flavours are delicate (for example, Shaoxing yellow wine) and should ideally be served warm: white alcohols are much stronger. They are made from corn, rice or more rarely from sorghum (like the famous Meiguilu, fragranced with fresh rose petals). Traditional grape wine is equally made in China and resembles our fortified wines. As for grape wines made according to western processes, they are becoming more and more popular with the Chinese, even if the quality is somewhat not so satisfactory. Good wine is very expensive in China.

Soft drinks, colas and other non-alcoholic drinks are sold everywhere. You should be aware that fruit juices are usually sweeter and have only a little fruit flavour. Don't be taken aback if you are served hot water during a meal: consumption of cold water is not common in China and it is a way of showing the water has been boiled and that it is safe to drink.

Entertainment

Sporting and activities

▶ Golf

Golf courses began appearing some ten years or so ago on the outskirts of Beijing and Shanghai, under the impetus of Western residents and foreign investors.

▶ Daily exercise

To better understand the Chinese people's relationship to the body, there's nothing better than to go for a walk in a park in a town at dawn: all ages rub shoulders with all types of music playing in the background (and even in silence) to perform healthy exercise: *taijiquan* (tai chi in English, a series of slow movements) *qigong* (exercises based on breathing and concentration). On the street gym equipment allows everyone to exercise at any time during the day. In the evening couples meet up in the street, put their sound system on the ground and start dancing a tango or jive...

▶ Ping-pong

The most popular sport in China, ping-pong sweeps through hotels and homes: most have a room reserved for it with bats available at receptions. A good way to make links with the Chinese.

▶ Hiking

Climbing the most famous mountains is a spiritual quest, one of the greatest moments in a Chinese person's life. It symbolises the communion with nature. All the historic tourist massifs (Huangshan, Huashan, Putuoshan, etc.) are equipped with safe and well maintained stone paths forming endless stairs. The important thing is to profit from the views of the countryside and vegetation.

Cultural life

▶ Shows

Opera, circus, theatre, concerts: opportunities to discover Chinese culture are many and will show you all its riches. The Chinese public know how to be expressive and demanding at the same time, performances are rarely followed in silence. Warning: Evening performances usually start at 7pm and you must arrive at least 30

minutes before. Reservations can be made locally, a long time in advance (several months sometimes).

▶ *Parlour games*

Another strong part of Chinese cultural life is games (a game of go or Chinese checkers, Chinese chess, mah-jong, etc.). In China you will often come across Chinese playing by the street.

Night life

▶ *Information*

You can obtain free magazines detailing places to go, fashionable bars, the most popular discos, cinemas and screening times, etc.

Some of these publications bring out national editions listing other places too.

In Beijing: *That's Beijing*, *City Weekend*, *Metro*, *High Mag*, etc.

► *Where to go*

In Beijing, places for a night out can be found mainly at Shichahai, on the banks of the lakes, in Chaoyang, near the park of the same name and in Sanlitun.

Holidays, festivals and events

Chinese life beats to the rhythm of religious and traditional festivals which stretch out along the lunar calendar. Festivals and international events make their appearance, principally in Shanghai and Beijing and surrounding tourist areas.

Here is a selection of these events. For further information consult the website of the National Administration for Tourism.

Spring Festival (1st day of the 1st lunar month/mid of January to mid of February): It corresponds to the Chinese New Year, the most important celebration of the year and is celebrated as a family. Adults offer New Year gifts to children, debts are repaid, and people put on their Sunday best to start the year well. Firecrackers and fireworks light up the nights right up to Lantern Festival.

Lantern Festival (15th day of the 1st lunar month/February or March): Temples, parks and main thoroughfares are decorated by thousands of paper lanterns which, according to tradition, let in the good spirits and chase away the bad ones. A spectacle celebrated around China.

Tomb Sweeping Day (usually 5th April): Families sweep the tombs of their ancestors and make offerings: wreathes, false "ghost" money.

Dragon Boat Festival (5th day of the 5th lunar month/June): In memory of the death of the patriotic poet Qu Yuan (around 340-278 BC), drowned in the Yangtze River. Dragon boat races are organised along the rivers and lakes, particularly beautiful in the Hangzhou region.

Mid-autumn Festival (15th day of the 8th lunar month/end of September): The Chinese come to admire the brilliance of this night under the full moon in parks and gardens, opened especially, savouring "mooncake" (月 饼 , yuèbǐng) stuffed with nuts and sesame seeds. Fireworks in big towns.

Shopping

Bargaining

In China bargaining is the rule, except in supermarkets and State-owned shops. It's carried on in good humour if on top of it all there is an added smile and some patience. Warning though, the Chinese are masters in the art of negotiation! To give you some idea of the going prices, watch the transactions going on around you and the money exchanged.

Arts and crafts

▶ *Calligraphy*

To practice calligraphy requires four elements, the "four treasures of the study": paper, ink, an ink stone and a brush.

Calligraphy can be bought all over: in the touristiest thoroughfares, you will be accosted by young artists offering to sell you their works.

▶ *Ceramics*

Celadon, "blue and white" porcelain, "famille rose"... Ceramics is a very ancient art in China. You can find numerous shops everywhere which offer ceramics of every style and price.

▶ *Silk*

In China, the country where the most noble of all materials was invented, you can buy silk at very reasonable prices, compared with what you pay in Europe. Silks coming from the towns of Hangzhou and Suzhou are the most well-known.

Ask the salesperson on the silk markets to make you a dress to measure: they can have it done in a day or two.

Other purchases

▶ *Electronic goods*

They are much cheaper in China, and specialist shopping centres in

Beijing, attract a large amount of foreigners. Note all the same that guarantees in China are not systematically accepted in your own country: have a good think before making your mind up.

▶ *Clothes*

The largest textile producer in the world sells at unbeatable prices: have whatever clothes made from head to toe. Other than standardised clothes exported to every corner of the globe, you can have a *qipao*, the famous slit dress, a ladie's top with a cross fastening or a traditional blouse with a Mao-style collar.

Where to shop

▶ *Markets*

Flea markets, bird and plant markets, night markets... They are many and of every sort. You can do a shopping at the lowest cost, but be warned: often the goods are of lesser quality!

Sending your purchases home

Small shops do not have a shipping service. You will have to make use of the Chinese postal service which is generally reliable. However, in large towns, antiques or furniture shops can take care of sending your most bulky purchases by air freight (very fast) or by container (slower, but cheaper).

Your flight ticket usually allows you to send bulky bags by air freight (above the 20kg allowance) by paying a supplement (Air France Cargo, Air China Cargo...). You must deposit these bags in a warehouse close to the airport 2 to 3 days before departure.

Getting by in Chinese

Pinyin

Pinyin is the phonetic transliteration of Chinese in the Latin alphabet. Taught in schools, it is relatively well known by young people and in urban populations. Nevertheless, these people very quickly forget the particulars of the tone and

frequently get the letters wrong. It can notably allow you to be understood when you are asking the way. Mastering pinyin will open Chinese doors to you and a number of publications use this as a basis. General rules: vowels are pronounced and Chinese is nasalized.

There are altogether 21 initials in Chinese pinyin:

b: like "b" in "bed" (unaspirated, voiceless)

p: like "p" in "peach" (aspirated, voiceless)

m: like "m" in "meat"

f: like "f" in "foot"

d: like "d" in "day" (unaspirated)

t: like "t" in "tea" (aspirated)

n: like "n" in "need"

l: like "l" in "leaf"

g: like "g" in "get" (unaspirated)

k: like "k" in "kill" (aspirated)

h: like "h" in "hen"

j: close to "j" in "jeep"(without protruding the lips) (unaspirated, voiceless)

q: close to "ch" in "cheap"(without protruding the lips) (aspirated, voiceless)

x: close to "sh" in "shirt" (voiceless)

zh: like "dr" in "drink" (unaspirated)

ch: like "ch" in "match" (aspirated)

sh: close to "sh" in "shy"

r: close to "r" in "roll"

z: like "ds" in "words"(unaspirated)

c: like "ts" in "rats" (aspirated)

s: like "s" in "sunday"

▶ *Compass points and elements of place*

Addresses—Addresses in this guide use Chinese terms: *Jie*, *Lu*…

The longest roads are divided into different parts: the Chinese give the compass point just before the qualifier; e.g *Nanjing Donglu: "dong"* means East and "*lu*" means Road; thus "the east part of Nanjing Road".

English	Pinyin	Chinese

Holding a conversation

English	Pinyin	Chinese
Good Morning	Nǐhǎo	你好
Good bye	Zàijiàn	再见
Please	Qǐng	请
Thank You	Xièxie	谢谢
You're welcome	Búyòng xiè	不用谢
Excuse me	Duìbuqǐ	对不起
Cheers!	Gānbēi !	干杯!
The bill	Mǎidān	买单
Is that okay?	Hǎo mɑ?	好吗?
Alright (OK)!	Hǎo de!	好的!
Very good	Hěn hǎo	很好
Is there a...?	Yǒu ... mɑ?	有……吗?
There is...	Yǒu...	有……
There isn't...	Méi yǒu...	没有……
How much does it cost?	Duōshǎo qián?	多少钱?
It's too expensive!	Tài guì le!	太贵了!
Where is ...?	... zài nǎli?	……在哪里?
I don't know.	Wǒ bù zhīdào.	我不知道。
I should like...	Wǒ yào...	我要……
I don't want it!	Wǒ bú yào!	我不要!
Please give me a...	Qǐng gěi wǒ...	请给我……
I want to go to...	Wǒ yào qù...	我要去……
I want to buy...	Wǒ xiǎng mǎi...	我想买……
I don't understand.	Wǒ tīng bu dǒng.	我听不懂。
How do you say this in Chinese?	Hànyǔ zěnme shuō?	汉语怎么说?
What does this mean?	Zhè shì shénme yìsi?	这是什么意思?
Speak more slowly please.	Qǐng shuō màn yì diǎnr.	请说慢一点儿。
Can you write it down for me?	Nǐ kěyǐ xiě yí xià mɑ?	你可以写一下吗?
What is your nationality?	Nǐ shì nǎguó rén?	你是哪国人?
I am English.	Wǒ shì yīngguó rén.	我是英国人。
I am French.	Wǒ shì fǎguó rén.	我是法国人。

GENERAL PRACTICAL INFORMATION

English	Pinyin	Chinese
I am American.	Wǒ shì měiguó rén.	我是美国人。
I am Australian.	Wǒ shì àodàlìyà rén.	我是澳大利亚人。
What's your name?	Nǐ jiào shénme míngzi?	你叫什么名字?
My name is...	Wǒ jiào...	我叫……
When?	Shénme shíhòu?	什么时候?
What?	Shénme?	什么?
Who?	Shéi?	谁?
What time is it?	Jǐdiǎn zhōng le?	几点钟了?
Is it possible to...?	Kěyǐ... ma?	可以……吗?
It's possible.	Kěyǐ.	可以。
It's not possible.	Bù kěyǐ.	不可以。

Getting around, visiting

North	běi	北
South	nán	南
West	xī	西
East	dōng	东
Centre	zhōng	中
Northeast	dōngběi	东北
Northwest	xīběi	西北
Southeast	dōngnán	东南
Southwest	xīnán	西南
Square	guǎngchǎng	广场
Road	lù	路
Avenue	dàjiē	大街
Boulevard	dào	道
Street	jiē	街
Alley	xiàng	巷
Gate	mén	门
Bridge	qiáo	桥
Building	lóu	楼
Mountain	shān	山
River	hé	河

English	Pinyin	Chinese
River	jiāng	江
Lake	hú	湖
Sea	hǎi	海
Wood/Forest	lín	林
Buddhist temple	sì	寺
Garden	yuán	园
Palace	gōng	宫
Station	zhàn	站
Embassy	dàshǐguǎn	大使馆
Village	xiāngcūn	乡村
City/Town	chéngshì	城市
Country	guójiā	国家
Teahouse	cháguǎn	茶馆
Hospital	yīyuàn	医院
Post office	yóujú	邮局
Police	jǐngchá	警察
How do you get to...?	Dào... zěnme zǒu?	到……怎么走?
I'm lost.	Wǒ mílù le.	我迷路了。
I'm looking for...	Wǒ zhǎo...	我找……
Here	zhèlǐ	这里
Over there	nàlǐ	那里
Near	jìn	近
Far	yuǎn	远

Daily life

Drink	hē	喝
Eat	chīfàn	吃饭
Go shopping	mǎi dōngxi	买东西
Toilet	cèsuǒ	厕所
Telephone	diànhuà	电话
I/We	wǒ/wǒmen	我 / 我们
You	nǐ/nǐmen	你 / 你们
He/She/They	tā/tā/tāmen	他 / 她 / 他们
Sir	xiānsheng	先生

English	Pinyin	Chinese
Madam	tàitai	太太
A lot	duō	多
A little	shǎo	少
Big	dà	大
Small	xiǎo	小
Old	lǎo	老
Young	niánqīng	年轻
Used	jiù	旧
New	xīn	新
Hot	rè	热
Cold	lěng	冷
Beautiful	hǎokàn	好看
Ugly	nánkàn	难看
Sweet	tián	甜
Sour	suān	酸
Ill	bìng	病
Expensive	guì	贵
Cheap	piányi	便宜
Rich	yǒuqián	有钱
Poor	qióng	穷
Easy	jiǎndān	简单
Difficult	nán	难
Clean	gānjìng	干净
Dirty	zāng	脏
Quick	kuài	快
Slow	màn	慢
Fat	pàng	胖
Thin	shòu	瘦

The family

Parents	fùmǔ	父母
Dad	bàba	爸爸
Mum	māma	妈妈
Child	háizi	孩子

English	Pinyin	Chinese
Daughter	nǚ'er	女儿
Son	érzi	儿子
Grandfather	yéye	爷爷
Grandparents	zǔfùmǔ	祖父母
Husband	zhàngfu	丈夫
Wife	qīzi	妻子

Transport

Taxi	chūzūchē	出租车
Bus	gōnggòng qìchē	公共汽车
Underground/Subway	dìtiě	地铁
Bicycle	zìxíngchē	自行车
Rickshaw	huángbāochē	黄包车
Train	huǒchē	火车
Plane	fēijī	飞机
Airport	fēijīchǎng	飞机场
Ticket	piào	票
Baggage	xínglǐ	行李
Right	yòubian	右边
Left	zuǒbian	左边
Behind	hòumian	后面
In front	qiánmian	前面
Go straight on.	Yìzhí zǒu.	一直走。
Make a U-turn.	Wǎng huí zǒu.	掉头往回走。
We've arrived!	Dào le!	到了！
I would like to buy a ticket for...	Wǒ yào mǎi yìzhāng qù... de piào.	我要买一张去…… 的票。

Numbers

0	líng	零
1	yī	一
2	èr	二
3	sān	三

English	Pinyin	Chinese
4	sì	四
5	wǔ	五
6	liù	六
7	qī	七
8	bā	八
9	jiǔ	九
10	shí	十
11	shíyī	十一
19	shíjiǔ	十九
20	èrshí	二十
100	yìbǎi	一百
200	liǎngbǎi	两百
208	liǎngbǎi língbā	两百零八
500	wǔbǎi	五百
562	wǔbǎi liùshí'èr	五百六十二
1 000	yìqiān	一千
2 000	liǎngqiān	两千
10 000	yíwàn	一万
100 000	shíwàn	十万
1 000 000	yìbǎiwàn	一百万

Colours

English	Pinyin	Chinese
White	bái	白
Black	hēi	黑
Red	hóng	红
Yellow	huáng	黄
Blue	lán	蓝
Green	lǜ	绿
Brown	zōng	棕
Purple	zǐ	紫
Dark green	shēnlǜ	深绿
Light green	qiǎnlǜ	浅绿

English	Pinyin	Chinese
Time		
Morning	shàngwu	上午
Noon	zhōngwu	中午
Afternon	xiàwu	下午
Evening	wǎnshang	晚上
Yesterday	zuótiān	昨天
Today	jīntiān	今天
Tomorrow	míngtiān	明天
Now	xiànzài	现在
Hour	xiǎoshí	小时
Minute	fēnzhōng	分钟
Quarter	kè	刻
Monday	xīngqīyī	星期一
Tuesday	xīngqī'èr	星期二
Sunday	xīngqītiān	星期天
Weekend	zhōumò	周末
What time is it now?	Xiànzài jǐdiǎn?	现在几点?
What day is today?	Jīntiān xīngqī jǐ?	今天星期几?
What is the date today?	Jīntiān jǐyuè jǐhào?	今天几月几号?
It is August 8th.	Bāyuè bāhào.	八月八号。

English	Pinyin	Chinese
At the restaurant		
Restaurant	fànguǎn	饭馆
Menu	càidān	菜单
Chopsticks	kuàizi	筷子
Fork	chāzi	叉子
Knife	dāozi	刀子
Spoon	sháozi	勺子
Glass/cup	bēizi	杯子
Bottle	píngzi	瓶子
What are your specialities?	zhèli yǒu shénme tèsè cài?	这里有什么特色菜?
To order.	Diǎncài.	点菜。
It's delicious.	Hǎochī jí le.	好吃极了。
The bill.	Mǎidān.	买单。

English	Pinyin	Chinese
At the hotel		
Hotel	fàndiàn	饭店
Room	fángjiān	房间
Bathroom	yùshì	浴室
I'd like to book a double room.		
	Wǒ yào dìng yìjiān shuāngrén fángjiān.	我要订一间双人房间。
How much does the room cost?	Zhèjiān fángjiān duōshao qián?	这间房间多少钱?

English	Pinyin	Chinese

At the market

Market	shìchǎng	市场
I'd like to buy...	Wǒ xiǎng mǎi...	我想买……
How much does it cost?	Yígòng duōshao qián?	一共多少钱?
It's too expensive.	Tài guì le.	太贵了。
Cheaper please.	Piányi yìdiǎnr.	便宜一点。

At the bank

Bank	yínháng	银行
Exchange money	huànqián	换钱
Chinese money	rénmínbì	人民币
Euro	ōuyuán	欧元
Swiss Franc	ruìshì fǎláng	瑞士法郎
Dollar	měiyuán	美元
Passport	hùzhào	护照

At the hospital

Hopital	yīyuàn	医院
Doctor	yīshēng	医生
Traditional Chinese medicine	zhōngyào	中药
Western medicine	xīyào	西药
Have a cold	gǎnmào	感冒
Have a headache	tóuténg	头疼
Have a fever	fāshāo	发烧
Comfortable	shūfu	舒服
See a doctor	kànbìng	看病
Have an injection	dǎzhēn	打针
What's the matter?	Zénme le?	怎么了?
Do you think I should be hospitalized?	Nín kàn wǒ xūyào zhùyuàn ma?	您看我需要住院吗?
Have a good rest.	Hǎohao xiūxi.	好好休息。

Getting to Beijing   46

Getting around   49

2008: Beijing Olympics   56

How to get about   60

Useful addresses   61

Where to stay   63

Where to eat   74

Going out for a drink   82

Things to do   87

History   106

DISCOVER BEIJING

Introduction to Beijing

Capital of Imperial China from the 13th century to the 20th century, then capital of the People's Republic of China from 1949, Beijing combines historical importance, population density, immense geographical size...and rapid change, speeded up even more by the 2008 Olympic Games. In this city of a thousand faces, we see a coexistence of traditional and modern elements in a framework of perpetual motion. Tiny alleyways where the smell of cooking drifts by, internal courtyards of the disappearing *siheyuan* and over-sized marble buildings around Tian'anmen Square, small Muslim quarters in the shadow of commercial banks, mass tourism and Chaoyang's avant-garde art galleries: Beijing is above all something to make your head turn, a collection of images where modern travellers look for their small share of experiences, a collection of mystery. The Chinese capital changes at a crazy pace. From one day to the next, a narrow *hutong* can turn into an avenue, a one-hundred year old dumpling restaurant into a DVD shop, a barber's shop into an Internet café... Don't come loaded with preconceived ideas that would only lead to disappointment.

Getting to Beijing

By air

Beijing Capital Airport has 3 terminals by the time of the 2008 Olympics. It is situated 25 kilometres northeast of the city in Chaoyang District. Tel(010) 64541100. http://en.bcia.com.cn/

By taxi, give yourself about 45 minutes to get to the city centre by expressway, though give more time during the rush hour. The journey costs about 80 yuan, including 10 yuan Road Toll. If you're carrying baggage or tired by the flight or jet-lagged, this is without doubt the most comfortable way to start your stay and get to the city centre.

The **Airport Shuttle Bus,** 24-Hour Hotline: (010) 64594375/64594376 (mandarin only). http://en.bcia.com.cn/traffic-manual/airport-bus.shtml

Four shuttle services, departing from the airport (stationed on the arrivals level), to city centre (journey time: from about 45 minutes to 90 minutes). 16 yuan. Leaves every 15 to 30 minutes.

Line 1: to Fangzhuang

6am—7:30pm

Stops: 1. Liangmaqiao; 2. Hujialou; 3. Dabeiyao (World Trade Centre); 4. Panjiayuan; 5. Shilihe (King Wing Hot Spring International Hotel); 6. Fangzhuang (Guiyou Shopping Mall);

Line 2: to Xidan

7am—the last flight

Stops: 1. Sanyuanqiao; 2. Dongzhimen; 3. Dongsishitiao Bridge; 4. Xidan (Civil Aviation Building);

Line 3: to Beijing Railway Station

7:30am—the last flight

Stops: 1. Yuyang Hotel; 2. Dongdaqiao (bypassed after 10:30pm); 3. Chaoyangmen; 4. Yabaolu; 5. Beijing Railway Station;

Line 4: to Gongzhufen

7am—11pm

Stops: 1. China International Exhibition Centre; 2. Xibahe; 3. Anzhen Bridge; 4. Madian Bridge; 5. Beitaipingzhuang; 6. Jimen Bridge; 7. Friendship Hotel; 8. Beijing TV Station; 9. Zizhu Bridge; 10. Hangtian Bridge; 11. Gongzhufen (Xinxing Hotel);

Line 5: to Zhongguancun

8:30am—9:30pm

Stops: 1. Wangjing (Huajiadi); 2. Xiaoying; 3. Asian Games Village (Anhui Bridge); 4.Xueyuan Bridge; 5. Zhongguancun Bridge.

Now there is an underground line connecting the airport to Dongzhimen Station.

Aeroflot, 1st Floor, Jinglun Hotel, 3 Jianguomenwai Dajie, Chaoyang District.

俄罗斯航空　朝阳区建国门外大街 3 号京伦大厦 1 层

Tel (010)65002412

www.aeroflot.com.

Air China, Civil Aviation Building, 15 Xi Chang'an Jie, Xicheng District.

国航　西城区西长安街 15 号民航大厦

Tel 8008101111

www.airchina.com.cn

Other address: Jingxin Building, A2 Dongsanhuan Beilu, Chaoyang District.

朝阳区东三环北路甲 2 号京信大厦

Tel (010) 64661697

China Eastern, 12 Xinyuanxili Dongjie, Chaoyang District.

东方航空　朝阳区新源西里东街 12 号

Tel (010) 64680066

www.ce-air.com

Dragon Air, Room 1710, Henderson Centre, Office Tower 1, 18 Jianguomennei Dajie, Dongcheng District.

港龙航空　东城区建国门内大街恒基中心 1710 室

Tel (010) 65182533

www.dragonair.com

Shanghai Airlines, 22th floor, Kunsha Centre, 16 Xinyuanli, Chaoyang District.

Map I, E2.

上海航空　朝阳区新源里 16 号琨莎中心 22 层

Tel (010)64569019/8008201018

www.shanghai-air.com

Air France, Rooms 1606—1611, Building 1 Kuntai International Mansion, 12 Chaoyangmenwai Dajie, Chaoyang District.

Map IV

法国航空　朝阳区朝阳门外大街 12 号昆泰国际大厦 1 号楼 1606—1611 房

Tel 4008808808

www.airfrance.com

Air Canada, Room C201, Lufthansa Centre, 50 Liangmaqiao Lu, Chaoyang District.

加拿大航空　朝阳区亮马桥路 50 号燕莎中心 C201 室

Tel (010) 64682001

www.aircanada.ca

British Airways, Room 210, Scitech Tower, 22 Jianguomenwai Dajie, Chaoyang District.

英国航空　朝阳区建国门外大街 22 号赛特大厦 201 室

Tel (010) 85115599

www.britishairways.com

KLM Royal Dutch Airlines, Rooms 1609-1611, Kuntai International Mansion, 12 Chaoyangmenwai Dajie, Chaoyang District.

荷兰皇家航空　朝阳区朝外大街 12 号昆泰国际大厦 1609—1611 房

Tel 4008808222

www.klm.com

Lufthansa Airlines, Rooms S101 and C202, Lufthansa Centre Office Building, 50 Liangmaqiao Lu, Chaoyang District.

德国汉莎航空　朝阳区亮马桥路 50 号燕莎中心办公楼 S101 和 C202 室

Tel (010) 64688838

www.lufthansa.com

By train

Train tickets cannot be purchased more than 10 days before departure, either at the station itself, at travel agencies or online at www.51piao.com/train or by telephone: 68056669/64656699

Central Station (Beijing Railway Station), Beijing Zhan, Chongwen District

MapI, D3

北京站　崇文区

Tel (010) 51821114

This is the main railway station. Departures for the Trans-Siberian and Trans-Manchurian lines.

West Station, Xike Zhan, Lianhuachi Donglu, Xuanwu District.
MapI, C3
西客站　宣武区莲花池东路
Tel (010) 51826253, 24/7 mandarin only
Trains to Western and Southern China. Departures every other day at 10am to Hong Kong (journey time 27 hours).

By bus

Dongzhimen Coach Station, Dongzhimenwai Xiejie, Dongcheng District.
东直门长途汽车站　东城区东直门外斜街
Tel (010) 64673094
6am–7pm
This is the main coach station. Departures to the Great Wall and coaches to other provinces.

Liuliqiao Coach Station, 1 Liuliqiao Nanli, Fengtai District.
六里桥长途汽车站　丰台区六里桥南里1号
Tel (010) 63861264
6:30am–10pm
Departures to Hebei, Henan, Shanxi and Fujian provinces.

Zhaogongkou Coach Station, Zhaogongkou Qiao, 34 Nan sanhuan Zhonglu, Xuanwu District.
赵公口长途汽车站　宣武区南三环中路34 号赵公口桥
Tel (010) 67229491
5:30am–7:30pm
Departures to Tianjin, Hebei, Zhejiang and other southern provinces.

Getting around

It's hard to outline the geography of Beijing such is the capital's current rapid change. There are today not one, but several centres. Six ring roads surround the city and constitute so many landmarks for Beijingers. Here we have simply chosen to divide it up around the most important historic monuments and the liveliest quarters. We have grouped together tourist sites, museums, temples and other places of interest around 6 "walking tours", to which we have added 2 excursions around Beijing (to the Summer Palace and the Great Wall).

Warning: in Beijing to get around you have to orientate yourself in relation to the North-South and East-West axes. These form the shape of the city and lend the streets their names. Handy tip, bring a compass with you; you'll find it very useful.

Walking Tour 1: The Forbidden City and Wangfujing
Maps II & III
Geographical, political and historic centre of Beijing. Around Tian'anmen Square are arranged the National People's Congress, the National Museum of China, and the Forbidden City Museum; at the

centre stands the Chairman Mao Memorial Hall and the Monument to the People's Heroes. There are shopping streets of Dashilan (or Dashilan in the local dialect) and Liulichang openning out. Here is also the old Beijing railway station and the very interesting, but less well-known, Beijing Planning Exhibition Hall. Large building works have been ongoing in the Qianmen area since 2006. The restored (or even rebuilt) quarter was openned up on August 7, 2008.

To the north of the Forbidden City are the imperial parks of Coal Hill (Jingshan) and Beihai, as well as the China Art Gallery. Along the City, leaving from Tian'anmen Square, green spaces of Changpuhe have been created as well as Nanchizi Dajie, destined to become a chic residential quarter with a traditional appearance. To the east you can find Donghuamen night market, the shopping street of Wangfujing, Dongsi Dajie which you can follow to where it meets Dongdan to reach the wide Chang'an Jie.

Walking Tour 2: Around Deshengmen
MapIII

This area, consisting of a historic centre, has become a simply unavoidable part of the night-life scene, by reason of its attraction in bringing together the three Imperial Lakes, with the traditional architecture in harmony with the numerous

bars and restaurants. Early in the morning (around 6am to 7am in summer), Beijingers go for a walk, do physical exercises, sing, go fishing here... At midday the passers-by nonchalantly saunter by. In the evening, a completely different atmosphere rules the water's edge: neon-lit bars, deafening music...

Walking Tour 3: Sanlitun and Chaoyang District

MapIV

Chaoyang district is very lively, here are restaurants offering all types of food from all over the world and "Bar Street", the bustling centre of night life. It's also a commercial quarter, with Yaxiu Market and

numerous fashion stores. Not far away, around the Workers' Stadium, the tendency is for extravagantly decorated restaurants and night clubs. It's the part of the city where it's all happening with Spas, massage centres and other sophisticated leisure places.

Walking Tour 4: Around Dongzhimen
Maps I& IV

This is a developing quarter where breathtakingly designed skyscrapers soar out of sight. It's a residential and business quarter; there are major hotels, luxury apartments, commercial centres and restaurants. In the eastern half of this quarter, "Ghost Street" is a favourite place to get refined and cheap food at the restaurants along the road.

Walking Tour 5: South of Qianmen
Map I

This quarter features a lot of Beijing's grand historical buildings, such as the Temple of Heaven and the Source of Law Temple. The popular *hutong* close to Qianmen, are gradually being replaced by wide avenues and new renovating quarters.

Walking Tour 6: West Beijing
MapII

Try to escape the tourist gaze. Nevertheless, if you have time, some sights merit attention: the Millennium Museum, the Military Museum, Xidan shopping centre. The National Opera House built by Paul Andreu has opened. To the southwest stretches out a working-class quarter where

several secondary temples, but nevertheless worthy of interest, exist in the midst of the dwellings. To the northwest you have Yuanmingyuan and Summer Palace, as well as the university quarter.

Walking Tour 7: Around Beijing

Yuanmingyuan and Summer Palace and the Fragrant Hills Park can be found 15 kilometres or so west of Beijing. These three sites, despite destruction, ruin and the ravage of time, have perfectly preserved their imperial majesty. This is an excellent chance to find calm and tranquillity when the bustle of the capital becomes too much.

Walking Tour 8: The Great Wall and the Imperial Tombs

Finally, it would be a shame to not spare a day, or even half a day visiting the Great Wall. On the way back you could also discover the Ming and Qing Tombs, sophisticated and spectacular constructions above and below ground.

Beijing is a city on the move where each day sees change. We have tried to choose those places that have stood the test of time, but the city changes with such speed that some of the sites mentioned may no longer exist at the time of your visit. Several English language magazines, like *That's Beijing*, *City Weekend*, *Beijing Talk*, or even *Time Out Beijing*, are available free in bars and hotels. They will give you the chance to discover the up-to-date places as well as cultural events.

2008: Beijing Olympics

Beijing, as well as six other Chinese cities (Tianjin, Hong Kong, Shanghai, Qingdao, Shenyang and Qinhuangdao) welcome the Games of the 29th Olympiad. For this occasion the capital gets a new skin: some quarters have been renovated (in particular to the south of Qianmen), public transport has been considerably improved, monuments restored, international construction completed…30 to 40 million dollars has been raised to restructure Beijing. The opening ceremony takes place at 8:08 pm on 8th August 2008 (the number 8 is lucky in China), and ends on 24th August. For information (in English) look at the official website http://en.eijing2008.cn/.

The theme for 2008 Olympics is "One World One Dream", which expresses the common wishes of people all over the world, inspired by the Olympic ideals, to strive for a bright future of Mankind. Despite the differences in colors, languages and races, we share the charm and joy of the Olympic Games, and seek for the ideal of Mankind in peace together. As we know, every emblem of the Olympics tells a story. The Beijing 2008 Olympic Games emblem "Chinese Seal, Dancing Beijing" is not only filled with Beijing's hospitality and hopes, but also carries the city's commitment to the world. Fuwa are the Official Mascots of the Beijing 2008 Olympic Games. Each of Fuwa has a rhyming two-syllable name, which is a traditional way of expressing affection for children in China. Beibei is the Fish, Jingjing is the Panda, Huanhuan is the Olympic Flame, Yingying is the Tibetan Antelope and Nini is the Swallow. Fuwa act as young ambassadors for the Olympic Games. When you put their names together, it says "Bei Jing Huan Ying Ni", which means "Welcome to Beijing".

Olympic Sports Venues (in Beijing)

Olympic venues	Chinese name	Competition
National Stadium	国家体育场	Opening ceremony, Closing ceremony, Athletics, Football
National Aquatics Center	国家游泳中心	Swimming, Diving, Synchronized Swimming
National Indoor Stadium	国家体育馆	Trampoline, Handball, Gymnastics Rhythmic
Beijing Shooting Range Hall	北京射击馆	Shooting
Beijing Olympic Basketball Gymnasium	北京奥林匹克篮球馆	Basketball
Laoshan Velodrome	老山自行车馆	Cycling
Shunyi Olympic Rowing-Canoeing Park	顺义奥林匹克水上公园	Rowing, Canoe/Kayak Flatwater, Canoe/Kayak Slalom
China Agricultural University Gymnasium	中国农业大学体育馆	Wrestling
Peking University Gymnasium	北京大学体育馆	Table Tennis
Beijing Science and Technology University Gymnasium	北京科技大学体育馆	Judo, Taekwondo
Beijing University of Technology Gymnasium	北京工业大学体育馆	Badminton, Gymnastics Artistic
Beijing Olympic Green Tennis Court	北京奥林匹克公园网球中心	Tennis
Olympic Sports Centre Stadium	奥体中心体育场	Football, Modern Pentathlon
Olympic Sports Centre Gymnasium	奥体中心体育馆	Handball
Beijing Workers' Stadium	北京工人体育场	Football
Beijing Workers' Gymnasium	北京工人体育馆	Boxing
Capital Indoor Stadium	首都体育馆	Volleyball
Fengtai Sports Centre Softball Field	丰台体育中心垒球场	Softball

Olympic venues	Chinese name	Competition
Yingdong Natatorium of National Olympic Sports Center	英东游泳馆	Aquatics, Water Polo, Modern Pentathlon
Laoshan Mountain Bike Course	老山山地自行车场	Cycling
Beijing Shooting Range CTF	北京射击场飞碟靶场	Shooting
Beijing Institute of Technology Gymnasium	北京理工大学体育馆	Volleyball
Beijing University of Aeronautics and Astronautics Gymnasium	北京航空航天大学体育馆	Weightlifting
Fencing Hall of National Convention Center	国家会议中心击剑馆	Fencing, Modern Pentathlon
Beijing Olympic Green Hockey Stadium	北京奥林匹克公园曲棍球场	Hockey
Beijing Olympic Green Archery Field	北京奥林匹克公园射箭场	Archery
Beijing Wukesong Sports Centre Baseball Field	北京五棵松体育中心棒球场	Baseball
Chaoyang Park Beach Volleyball Ground	朝阳公园沙滩排球场	Beach Volleyball
Laoshan Bicycle Moto Cross(BMX)Venue	老山小轮车赛场	Cycling(BMX)
Triathlon Venue	铁人三项赛场	Triathlon
Road Cycling Course	公路自行车赛场	Cycling(road race)

How to get about

Pre-paid travel cards "市政交通一卡通"(shìzhèng jiāotōng yìkǎtōng) are on sale in underground stations. They can be used on the bus, in the underground and (theoretically) in taxis.

▶ By car

International driving licences are not recognised in China. You must obtain a licence to be able to drive in the territory. If you want to get around by car, you can hire a vehicle with driver (it's relatively cheap), either by going to a hire-car agency (600—800 yuan per day), or directly negotiate a daily rate with a taxi driver (300 yuan per day).

Hire Cars—Beijing First Auto Rental, Tel (010) 66167000. 8:30am—5pm.

Hertz, Tel 8008108883/(010) 65958109, 9am—6pm, www.hertz.com.

▶ By bicycle

A good way to get to know the city and to mingle in with the masses, you need to be careful! Beijing is a flat city and does not pose any particular problems getting around by bicycle. It's possible to hire bicycles by the day or half-day in most hotels or at hire-shops in tourist areas.

Bicycle Rental, behind Di'anmen Department Store, Xicheng District. Tel (010) 64041336, extension 2414, 9am—8:30pm (30 yuan/day).

Bicycle Kingdom, B402-5, North Garden Office, Oriental Plaza, Wangfujing, Dongcheng District.

Tel (010) 85494541, 60—120 yuan/day, www.bicyclekingdom.com.

▶ By taxi

The most practical way to get around the city! Very easy to find (there are more than 60 000 taxis in Beijing!), except when it's raining and sometimes during rush hour, and they are not expensive: a journey in the city centre costs about 15—20 yuan: 10 yuan for the first 3

kilometres, then 2 yuan per kilometres. After 11pm, night rate applies: 11 yuan for the first 3 kilometres, then 3 yuan per kilometres. Drivers could speak a little English and do all they can to give you a good service. To be certain to arrive at the right place, show the address written in Chinese, or better still, if you have a local network mobile phone, call the restaurant or hotel where you want to get to; they will directly tell the driver the route to follow. A final piece of advice: keep the receipt; it will enable you to find the car again if you leave something in the car.

▶ By bus

With a 1 yuan fare per journey, buses are the most economical means of transport. It is however slow and not that practical if you haven't mastered Chinese. If all the same you want to experience it, you can get information and bus timetables in English on the website, www.bjbus.com.

▶ By underground (subway)

Map p. 115

Quick, economical (2 yuan per journey) and very practical

during rush hour (morning between 8am and 10am, evening between 5pm and 7pm) to avoid hold-ups. Beijing's underground network will consist of 8 lines by summer 2008. Runs from 5am to 11pm.

Useful addresses

Tourism office

Tourist Hotline
24/7 and only in Chinese for the time being!
Tel (010) 65130828

Beijing Tourist Information Centre
Several outlets in the capital. Partly English information in leaflets and city maps.
www.bjta.gov.cn.

Beijing Tourist Information Centre Wangfujing
Map III, D3
10 Dengshikou Xijie, Dongcheng District.
东城区灯市口西街 10 号
Tel (010) 65123043
9am—5pm
The city centre outlet.

Beijing Tourist Information Centre Tiantan
Map I, D3.
3 Hufang Lu, Xuanwu District.
宣武区虎坊路 3 号
Tel (010) 63510018
9am—5pm
Close to the Temple of Heaven.

Beijing Tourist Information Centre Sanlitun
Map IV
27 Gongti Beilu, Chaoyang District.

朝阳区工体北路 27 号
Tel (010) 64176627
9:30am—5:30pm
In Sanlitun, the "Embassy Quarter".

Bank/Exchange

It's better to change your money on arrival at the Airport (the rate is about the same everywhere). In city you can also change money at large hotels (Peninsula or Novotel Peace, in the centre), or even in branches of the big banks, like Bank of China or CITIC, on the main roads (Wangfujing, Jianguomenwai, Sanlitun, Gongti, Tiantan…). But here you risk wasting a lot of time. There are also many ATMs which accept overseas cards, but not all work.

Bank of China, 1 Fuxingmennei Dajie, Xicheng District.
中国银行总行　西城区复兴门内大街 1 号
Tel (010) 95566

HSBC, Ground Floor, Block A, COFCO Plaza, 8 Jianguomennei Dajie, Chaoyang District.
汇丰银行　朝阳区建国门内大街 8 号
Tel (010)8008208878/4008208828

Post office

The Chinese Post office is very reliable. Mails for overseas arrive pretty quickly; allow for about 1 week. Postcards are stamped 4.5 yuan, letters 6 yuan. The postal colour is dark green;

it's the colour of all the Post Office shop fronts and the post boxes.

The International Post Office is on Yabao Lu, Chaoyang District
Map IV,A3
国际邮局　朝阳区雅宝路
Tel (010) 65128114
8am—6:30pm

Telephone

Beijing dialling code:

— 10 from overseas,

— 010 inside China.

There are telephone boxes for calling overseas at the international post office (see above), open 8am to midnight.

Internet

The majority of hotels offer Internet access. Cybercafés abound, but they disappear as quickly as they appear! Here are some of them:

Qianyi Internet Café
Map III, C4
3rd Floor, Old Railway Station Shopping Mall, Tian'anmen Guangchang, Dongcheng District.
前艺网络咖啡屋　东城区天安门广场老火车站商场 3 层
Tel (010) 67051722
9am—11pm

Closed Sunday. Very central in the old Beijing Railway Station building, south of Tian'anmen. It's quite expensive: 10 yuan/ 30 minutes.

Bars in Nanluogu Xiang
Map III, B-C1

In the Drum Tower and lakes quarter, almost all offer Wi-Fi access.

钟楼湖区南锣鼓巷

Bar Blu
Map IV, B2

4th Floor Tongli Studios, Sanlitun Beilu, Chaoyang District, Wi-Fi access.

朝阳区三里屯北路同里 4 楼

Emergencies/Health

Emergency number: 999.

Hospitals:
Sino-Japanese Hospital
Map I, D1

Hepingli Beikou, Yinghua Dongjie, Chaoyang District.

中日友好医院 朝阳区樱花东街和平里北口

Tel (010) 64222952
For Foreigners, (010) 64221122, ext. 3411 for emergencies.

Foreigner's reception Mon.—Fri. 8am—noon, 1pm—5pm, English-speaking staff and Western trained doctors.

Peking Union Medical College Hospital
Map III, D3-4

1 Shuaifuyuan Hutong, Dongcheng District.

北京协和医院 东城区帅府园胡同 1 号

Tel (010) 65295269 (foreigners reception), (010) 65295284 (emergencies)

Mon.—Fri. 8am—4:30pm. The best hospital in city offers a welcome service to foreigners, doctors trained in the West and English-speaking staff.

International Medical Center
Map IV, C1

Bureau S106, 1st Floor, Lufthansa Centre, 50 Liangmaqiao Lu, Chaoyang District.

北京国际医疗中心 朝阳区亮马河路 50 号燕莎中心

Tel (010) 64651561/2/3

Foreigners' clinic open 24/7, English-speaking staff and overseas doctors. The fees for consultations are quite high.

Chemists: Wangfujing Medicine Shop
Map III, D3

267 Wangfujing Dajie, Dongcheng District.

王府井医药器械公司 东城区王府井大街 267 号

Tel (010) 65249932
8:30am—9pm

Watsons
Map III, D4

Oriental Plaza, shop CC17, 1st floor.

屈臣氏 东方广场首层 CC17

Tel (010) 85186428
9am—9pm

Where to stay

In Beijing, the price of hotels can vary fourfold depending on the time of year: low season from Nov. to Jan., medium season from Feb. to Mar., high season from Apr. to Oct.. Thus you can benefit from interesting rates in high-class hotels in winter. Book several days in advance; it's another way of getting discounts. Word of warning, breakfast is not usually included in the room rate.

Around the Forbidden City and Wangfujing

▶ *Less than 300 yuan*

Jade International Youth Hostel ⑧
Map III, C3
5 Zhide Beixiang, Beiheyan Dajie, Dongcheng District.
智德青年宾馆　东城区北河沿大街智德北巷 5 号
Tel (010) 65259966
www.xihuahotel.com

114 beds in dormitories, from 40 yuan (8 beds) to 60 yuan (4 beds); in the hotel: 80 rooms, 280—480 yuan (depending on the season). Internet access. This establishment, which brings together Youth Hostel and hotel, is ideally situated at the heart of the *hutong*, a few steps from the Forbidden City and 5 minutes, walk from Wangfujing. Clean and well-maintained, the rooms are small, without charm, but functional and prices are extremely low for a tourist quarter. Showers in the corridor for the dorms. Large dining room (western and Chinese food) and a very comfortable lounge. Excursions can be arranged.
Bonus: if you book several days in advance they will pick you up at the station.

Saga Youth Hostel ⑲
Map III, E3
9 Shijia Hutong, Dongcheng District.
北京实佳青年宾馆　东城区史家胡同 9 号
Tel (010) 65272773

Dorms from 50 yuan (8 to 14 beds) to 60 yuan (4 to 5 beds); Room with private bathroom: doubles 180 yuan, triples 210 yuan. A good atmosphere reigns in this very central youth hostel, close to Wangfujing. Various services: Internet café, laundry, bicycle hire, excursions. Roof terrace.

▶ *From 300 to 500 yuan*

Jiao Lou Business Hotel ⑨
Map III, C2
33 Wusi Dajie, Dongcheng District.
北京角楼商务宾馆　东城区五四大街 33 号
Tel (010) 64025399

50 rooms. From 268 yuan in low season to 880 yuan in high season. New establishment with modern comforts, the Jiao Lou is situated the closest it can be to the Forbidden City, near to the Fine Arts Museum, in a still-preserved quarter. Service here is good. It's the ideal starting point for a typical Beijing stroll around the *hutong* or in Jingshan Park where retired people get together every weekend to sing traditional and revolutionary songs. All the rooms have free internet access, with some having views of the Forbidden City.

▶ *From 500 to 1 000 yuan*

Hao Yuan Hotel ⑥
Map III, E3
53 Shijia Hutong, Deng Shi Dong Kou, Dongcheng District.
好园宾馆　东城区灯市东口史家胡同 53 号

Tel (010) 65125557
www.haoyuanhotel.com

19 rooms. 760 yuan. Imperial and western food. Not far from the wide shopping street of Wangfujing and a few feet from lively Dongsi, this charming hotel has calm tranquillity and beauty. In a pretty house with 2 courtyards which also houses the Women's Association, there are comfortable rooms decorated in a traditional style, but flashy nonetheless. Those that look out onto the rear courtyard are particularly nice. The house also offers excursions and massage.

Booking is advised a week in advance.

Sihe Hotel ⑳
Map III, D3
5 Dengcao Hutong, Dongsi Nan dajie, Dongcheng District.
四合宾馆　东城区东四南大街灯草胡同 5 号
Tel (010) 51693555/65255280
www.sihehotel.com
12 rooms. From 750 to 1,580 yuan. Internet. A little difficult to find, this charming hotel is 10 minutes walk from Wangfujing, in a very picturesque *hutong*. The rooms look out onto the main courtyard of a *siheyuan* built during the Qing dynasty. Bicycle hire and small travel agency.

Hotel Kapok ⑩
Map III, C2
16 Donghuamen Dajie, Dongcheng District.
木棉花酒店　东城区东华门大街 16 号
Tel (010) 65259988
www.hotelkapok.com

89 rooms. From 1280 yuan in winter to 3180 yuan in summer. Wi-Fi. A couple of feet from the east gate of the Forbidden City and near Wangfujing, this hotel, conceived in a very Zen-like contemporary style with interior gardens, has a very good quality/price ratio. Superb dining room, bar, business and fitness centres. Booking advised.

Novotel Peace ⑬
Map III, D3
3 Jinyu Hutong,Wangfujing, Dongcheng District.
诺富特和平宾馆　东城区王府井金鱼胡同 3 号
Tel (010) 65128833
novotel@novotelpeacebj.com
388 rooms. From 675 to 3320 yuan according to the season. Very well located, a stone's throw away from the Forbidden City and the commercial crossroad of Wangfujing, the Novotel Peace is a meeting place for all French travellers. The rooms have been renovated and offer modern comfort. Moreover the hotel has a swimming pool and offers a French buffet as well as three restaurants.

▶ *More than 1,000 yuan*

Cuimingzhuang Hotel ④
Map III, C3
1 Nanheyan Dajie, Dongcheng District.
翠明庄宾馆　东城区南河沿大街 1 号
Tel (010) 58580909
www.jadegardenhotel.com
122 rooms. 1,200 yuan. Wi-Fi. Train tickets can be booked.

This grey stone building, constructed in the 1930s, was one of the offices of the Chinese Communist Party from 1946 and because of this is a protected historical building. Ideally situated between the east gate of the Forbidden City and the Donghuamen night market, near Wangfujing, the hotel does not put on a particular charm, but its rooms are very comfortable. Some look out onto the roofs of the traditional houses in this preserved *hutong*.

Beijing Hotel ②
Map III, D4
33 Dongchang'an Jie, Dongcheng District.
北京饭店　东城区东长安街 33 号
Tel (010) 65137766
605 rooms. From 3,500 yuan (prices shown in USD at reception). The Beijing Hotel is a vast complex located a couple of steps from Tian'anmen and the Forbidden City and its central building dates from the 1920's. The far east part of this construction dates from the 1970's. The rooms are very spacious here, some of which

overlook Chang'an Jie. There is a choice of several restaurants, among which a Steak House serves beef from Australia and a Western restaurant displays, at lunch, a sumptuous buffet. At the far west (the most recent part), Beijing's Grand Hotel is palatial. The rooms on the upper floors look out onto the roofs of the Forbidden City and Tian'anmen Square, the biggest in the world. A very pretty swimming pool. At the top, a restaurant and terrace overlooking the historical heart of the city.

Peninsula Palace ⑮

Map III, D3

8 Jinyu Hutong, Dongcheng District.

王府半岛饭店　王府井东城区金鱼胡同 8 号

Tel (010) 85162888

Upwards from 2,000 yuan. A very good address at the centre of the historical city, this hotel offers all the attributes of a palace. Swimming pool, spa, rooms delicately decorated, impeccable service, two very good restaurants (Chinese and international) and shopping malls where the biggest luxury brands line up.

Grand Hyatt ⑤

Map III, D4

1 Dongchang'an Jie, Dongcheng District.

东方君悦大酒店　东城区东长安街 1 号

Tel (010) 85181234

From 3,000 yuan. It is the fashionable address of the moment. It also has all the attributes of a palace: pretty rooms, spa, large pool. The hotel has equally under its roof a restaurant, the Made in China, where some of the most refined Chinese food in Beijing is served.

The Regent Beijing ⑦

Map III, D3

99 Jinbao Jie, Dongcheng District.

北京丽晶酒店　东城区金宝街 99 号

Tel (010) 85221888

www.regenthotels.com/beijingcn

500 rooms. From 1,800 yuan. This hotel is of high quality: incredibly vast foyer, very beautiful rooms, large pool, Spa...

Around Deshenmen

▶ *Less than 300 yuan*

Beijing Downtown Backpackers Accommodation ⑭

Map III, C1

85 Nanluogu Xiang, Ping'an Dajie, Dongcheng District.

北京东堂客栈　东城区平安大街南锣鼓巷 85 号

Tel (010) 84002429

downtown@backpackingchina.com

17 rooms. 50 beds; doubles: 150—190 yuan. A very clean youth hostel and ideally situated in a central *hutong*, close to the Drum Tower and the lakes. The rooms (single, double, triple, quadruple and dormitory) each have their own private bathroom; those which looked out over

the roofs of the old surrounding houses are particularly pleasant. The hostel also organises trips to the Great Wall. Free shuttle to the Airport if the booking is made at least 3 days in advance. An unbeatable quality/price combination in the centre.

▶ *From 300 to 500 yuan*

Youhao Guesthouse ㉒

Map III, D2

7 Houyuan'ensi, Dongcheng District.

友好宾馆　东城区后圆恩寺 7 号

Tel (010) 64031114

12 rooms. 392 yuan Japanese restaurant. Situated near the Drum Tower, this small calm hotel snuggling among the *hutong* was once the Beijing residence of Chiang Kai-shek.

Armed with this historical past, it offers a small number of rooms looking out onto a courtyard and its stone garden where it's nice to walk around. The rooms are comfortable without being pretty, the attraction of this hotel coming above all from its charming courtyard.

Hejingfu Hotel ⑦

Map III, D2

7 Zhangzizhong Lu, Dongcheng District.

和敬府宾馆　东城区张自忠路 7 号

Tel (010) 64032229

320 yuan. Breakfast not included. In a very calm quarter of traditional housing. A recent construction where the rooms, decorated in kitsch style, merits from being clean and cheap.

Ping An Fu Hotel ⑯

Map III, E2

100 Dongsi Shitiao, Dongcheng District.

平安福宾馆　东城区东四十条 100 号

Tel (010) 64016660

83 rooms. 768 yuan, excluding breakfast. Sauna and massage centre. Travel agency. A recent building imitating Ming and Qing traditional styles, this hotel is well located between the Yonghegong Lama Temple and the Forbidden City. It's all quite artificial-looking, but the rooms are comfortable and very tranquil.

Qomolangma Hotel ⑰

Map III, B1

149 Gulouxi Dajie, Xicheng District.

珠穆朗玛宾馆　西城区鼓楼西大街 149 号

Tel (010) 64018822
www.qomolangmahotel.com

100 rooms. From 580 to 1,080 yuan. Situated in the former Guanyue Temple with pretty, traditional architecture. The Qomolangma Hotel is a pleasant interlude in a preserved *hutong*. Modern comfortable rooms, simply decorated, are distributed between the main building and the different courtyards: take preferably a room looking onto a square courtyard. The Tibetan restaurant and planned excursions to Tibet and Mount Qomolangma are a reminder of the initial function of this building (the Chinese name for Everest).

Lu Song Yuan Hotel ⑫

Map III, D2

22 Banchang Hutong, Kuanjie, Dongcheng District.

侣松园宾馆　东城区宽街板厂胡同 22 号

Tel (010) 64040436/64011116
www.telhe-silk-road.com

DISCOVER BEIJING

58 rooms. From 388 to 21378 yuan. Wi-Fi Internet. Very well located in the centre, in an old *hutong*, this charming hotel is ideal for a stay. In an old *siheyuan* house around 5 square courtyards, the rooms are decorated in a traditional style. The small tearoom (which doubles as a cyber café) is pleasant. The restaurant serves good Beijing style food and the tables are put in the main courtyard in summer. The hotel also offers tai chi lessons and pedicab tours of the surrounding *hutong*... Booking 7 days in advance is advised.

Bamboo Garden Hotel ①

Map III, C1

24 Xiaoshiqiao Jiugulou Dajie, Xicheng District.

竹园宾馆　西城区旧鼓楼小石桥 24 号

Tel (010) 58520088
www.bbgh.com.cn

39 rooms. From 760 to 1,760 yuan, no breakfast. In a Chinese garden in the historical quarter, its modest size makes this hotel a haven of peace and an ideal starting point for walks in the surrounding *hutong*. Good quality

food and service. Pick the rooms at the back; they have balconies with pretty views across the stone garden and pavilion.

▶ *Over 1,000 yuan*

Red Capital Residence ⑱

Map III, E2

9 Dongsi Liutiao, Dongcheng District.

新红资宾馆　东城区东四六条 9 号

Tel (010) 84035308/84018886
www.redcapitalclub.com.cn

5 rooms. 1,125—1,700 yuan. A luxury *siheyuan,* this boutique hotel was opened by the owner of the famous Red Capital Club restaurant, mixing traditional and Mao period styles. In a magnificent courtyard, you can spend delightful times in a very high class environment. Don't miss its special features in the bar.

Sanlitun and Chaoyang District

▶ *Less than 300 yuan*

Apartments to rent

Tel 13141252001
www.locationsfrancophones-pekin.com

250 yuan/week. Take the plunge in Beijing whilst benefiting completely from western standards of living. These furnished one and two-roomed apartments are located in the Central Business District, close to China World Trade Centre (国 贸), 200 metres from the

underground station of Guomao (10 to 15 minutes by subway from Tian'anmen). Real pluses come with this benefit: two-way airport transfers in private car, loan of Chinese SIM during the whole stay.

Youyi Youth Hostel ⑥

Map IV, B2

43 Bei Sanlitun Nanlu, Chaoyang District.

友谊青年旅舍　朝阳区北三里屯南路 43 号

Tel (010) 64172632
www.poachers.com.cn

18 rooms. doubles: 180 yuan. Communal showers. Bicycle hire. Trips. Attached to the Poachers Bar, this youth hostel is at the heart of Beijing's nightlife, in Sanlitun. A very convivial atmosphere, but not the dream venue for a peaceful stay! Clean dorms and simple comfort. Plus points: Internet access (10 yuan/hour) and free laundry service.

Huatong International Youth Hostel ③

Map IV, B2

1 Gongti Beilu, Chaoyang District.

华通国际青年旅舍　朝阳区工体北路 1 号

Tel (010) 51909288
E-mail bj51909288@yahoo.com

50 rooms. Doubles: 280—320 yuan with bathroom; dormitory: from 70(6 beds) to 80(4 beds) yuan. Breakfast: 10 yuan. Laundry. This youth hostel, a member of Hostelling International, faces the Workers' Stadium, on the

same parking area as the Yugong yishan Bar. Currently the rooms are very clean. Ideally situated for party-goers.

Zhaolong Youth Hostel ⑦

Map IV, B2

2 Gongti Beilu, Chaoyang District.

兆龙青年旅舍　朝阳区工体北路 2 号

Tel (010) 65972666
E-mail YHZL@zhaolonghotel.com.cn

Doubles: 350 yuan with bathroom; dormitory: 60—80 yuan. Behind the luxury hotel Zhaolong, a place for people a low budget. A variety of services: Internet café, bicycle hire, tourist info… Very comfortable double rooms.

▶ *From 300 to 500 yuan*

Red House ④

Map IV, B2

10, Taipingzhuang, Chunxiu Lu, Dongzhimenwai Dajie, Chaoyang District.

瑞秀宾馆　朝阳区东直门外大街春秀路太平庄 10 号

Tel (010) 64167500
www.redhouse.com.cn

40 rooms. 400—600 yuan. Internet café. Breakfast included. Former youth hostel, where the rooms have been converted into mini-apartments, the Red House was opened by the owner of the Poachers and the Youyi (Friendship)Youth Hostel. "Hot-spot" for young travellers and night owls at the heart of the Expat Quarter. Set up in a large house, which is comfortable and reasonably

priced, the hotel offers several excursions, a free laundry service and Internet access: this all makes it a welcoming address.

▶ Over 1,000 yuan

City Hotel ②

Map IV, B2

4 Gongti Donglu, Chaoyang District.

城市宾馆 朝阳区工体东路 4 号

Tel (010) 65007799

220 rooms. 500—900 yuan. In a recently constructed tower block, the City Hotel is a meeting point in Sanlitun. Close to "Bar Street" and Yaxiu Market, one of the busiest shopping areas in the city. Modern comforts, without any particular charm. Good reduction if you book in advance (600 yuan).

China World Hotel ①

Map IV, B3

1 Jianguomenwai Dajie, Chaoyang District.

中国大饭店 朝阳区建国门外大街 1 号

Tel (010) 65052266

716 rooms. From 3,000 yuan. Right in the heart of the Central Business District (CBD), designed to demonstrate the ultra-modern face of the capital, with Soho's numerous buildings and creations designed by famous international architects, China World Trade Centre is a palace of the highest comfort. It has under its roof some of the best restaurants in the city serving foreign cuisine (the Italian Aria and Indian Taj Pavillion). It's a very lively complex where all the luxury brands are represented and where cultural events are often organised. Cheaper rooms are to be found behind at Beijng Traders' Hotel.

St Regis ⑤

Map IV, B4

21 Jianguomenwai Dajie, Chaoyang District.

北京国际俱乐部饭店 朝阳区建国门外大街 21 号

Tel (010) 64606688

From 3,150 yuan (prices advertised in USD at reception). Close to the Friendship Store, a very refined but modestly sized luxury hotel. Sunday Brunch, with as much caviar as you can eat. Spa and swimming pool open 24/7.

Around Dongzhimen

▶ Less than 300 yuan

Beijing Lama Temple Youth Hostel ③

Map III, D1

56 Beixinqiao Toutiao, Yonghegong Dajie, Dongcheng District.

北京雍和国际青年旅舍 东城区雍和宫大街北新桥头条 56 号

Tel (010) 64028663

E-mail lama_temple_hostel@yahoo.com.cn

14 rooms. 80 beds; doubles: 220 yuan; dormitory: 50—60 yuan.

A new youth hostel, very well located, in a *hutong* between the Lama Temple and Ghost Street. Caution: most doubles do not have windows. Numerous services available: bicycle hire, laundry, ticket booking, luggage deposit, internet (Wi-Fi)…

South of Qianmen

▶ Less than 300 yuan

Leo Hostel ⑪
Map III, C4
24 Buxiangzi Hutong, Qianmen Dajie.
兆阳宾馆　前门大街布巷子胡同 24 号
Tel (010) 67021560/13911927715 (Mobile)
www.leohostel.com
Reckon about 45 yuan for a bed in a dormitory, and 160 yuan for a double. This establishment, situated 500 metres south of Tian'anmen Square, has no charm and is not particularly comfortable but blends good location with attractive rates and excellent service. Leo opened this hotel in 2005 and continues to bring to it many improvements which contribute to creating a warm atmosphere. Original excursions are organised to the Great Wall.

Far East International Youth Hostel ②
Map II, C3
113 Tieshu XieJie, Xuanwu District.
远东国际青年旅舍　宣武区铁树斜街 113 号
Tel (010) 51958561
www.fareastyh.com
142 beds, 60—70 yuan dormitory beds (4 to 6 beds), 268 yuan doubles. Travel agency. Bicycle hire. The Far East International is attached to the Beijing Far East Hotel, located right opposite Tieshu XieJie (a section of the dormitories are elsewhere in the main hotel building). It occupies a traditional courtyard house, close to the tourist areas of Dashilan and Liulichang. Clean and prettily decorated. This is a charming address for people on a low budget. The courtyard, sometimes with several outdoor tables, is a haven in the heart of the city.

▶ From 300 to 500 yuan

Far East Hotel ①
Map II, C3
90 Tieshu Xiejie, Xuanwu District.
远东酒店　宣武区铁树斜街 90 号
Tel (010) 51958562
328—368 yuan. The faded façade of the Far East Hotel stands at the heart of the tourist districts of Dashilan and Liulichang. The whole place needs renovating but its location is perfect and the prices are within reach.

Where to eat

Around the Forbidden City and Wangfujing

▶ Less than 50 yuan

Wangfujing Xiaochi Jie ㉒
Map III, D4
Dashamao Hutong (opposite Oriental Plaza).
王府井小吃街　东城区大纱帽胡同（东方广场对面）

A small road off Wangfujing where you can eat on the run for a fistful of yuan: soups, noodles, meat kebabs—or, how about insects—delicious caramelised fruits (in the way toffee apples are made)...

Shun Yi Fu ⑱
Map III, D3
36-3 Ganyu Hutong (small road alongside, to the right, Wangfujing church), Dongcheng District.
顺一府饺子馆　东城区甘雨胡同36-3号（王府井教堂右侧小路）

Tel (010) 65281960

10:30am—10pm. A few yards from the big and noisy commercial thoroughfare of Wangfujing, a small local people's canteen, very lively at noon. The best *jiaozi* (stuffed dumplings) in the city: thirty odd different varieties, which, a rare thing in Beijing, aren't too fatty. The carrot and lamb and chicken and mushroom dumplings, as well as the *guotie* (grilled in Shanghai style) vegetarian and leek are very tasty. Try also tofu skin.

▶ From 100 to 200 yuan

Red Capital Club ⑰
Map III, E2
66 Dongsi Jiutiao, Dongcheng District.
新红资俱乐部　东城区东四九条66号
Tel (010) 64027150/84018886

6pm—11pm. This restaurant serves Imperial food. It's nestled in an old courtyard house. Prettily decorated. Booking recommended.

Fangshan Restaurant ④
Map III, C2
1 Wenjin Lu, Beihai Park (East Gate), Dongcheng District.
仿膳饭馆　东城区文津路1号北海公园内
Tel (010) 64011889

11am—2pm, 5pm—8pm. Menus from 198 yuan to 1,580 yuan; can be shared. One of the most famous restaurants in the city. A magic atmosphere in the middle of Beihai Park serving refined Imperial food. Access by boat.

▶ Over 200 yuan

The Courtyard ⑲

Map III, C3

95 Donghuamen Dajie, Dongcheng District.

四合院西餐厅　东城区东华门大街 95 号

Tel (010) 65268883

6pm—8pm. Hidden behind a wall of planted bamboo, several feet from the west gate of the Forbidden City, The Courtyard is one of the top chic places in the Chinese capital. This hybrid location, at the same time a fusion restaurant, contemporary art gallery and cigar lounge, is inspired by lawyer Handel Lee who is also the originator of the "Three on the Bund" in Shanghai and a witness to the reinvention of the Bund as a deluxe thoroughfare. The food, which blends western and oriental influences, is not at the highest point in terms of reputation and price. However, the atmosphere is very pleasant, particularly the smoking room on the first floor which offers views over the moat to the Forbidden City. Caution: the restaurant is only open in evenings, except Sunday when a brunch is offered at noon. Booking advised.

Tiandi Yijia ㉑

Map III, C4

140 Nanchizi Dajie, Dongcheng District.

天地一家　东城区南池子大街 140 号

Tel (010) 85115556

11am—2pm, 5pm—9:30pm. One of the most refined places in Beijing. Delicious imperial food. Stunningly decorated, modern and understated. The glazed duck is especially tasty. The restaurant is located in the street which runs along the east side of the Forbidden City and is part of the renovation programme designed to renew the old preserved quarters. You can go for a walk around the new Changpuhe gardens which contains the most beautiful varieties of peony in China.

Made in China ⑤

Map III, D 4

1st Floor of the Grand Hyatt Hotel, 1 Dongchang'an Jie, Dongcheng District.

长安一号 (东方君悦酒店一层)　东城区东长安街 1 号

Tel (010) 65109608

11:30am—2:30pm, 6pm—10pm. A staggering production and delicious food which comes from the specialities of the region. Guests see the chefs working at their table: preparing noodles and dumplings, cooking in a wok, chocolate fountains…

The Peking duck and "Beggar's Chicken" from Hangzhou (chicken cooked in a layer of earth for several hours) prepared like nowhere else. The sweet menu—rare thing in China—is very creative and also tasty.

Around Deshengnmen

▶ *Less than 50 yuan*

Ke Jia Cai ⑧

Map III, C2

Opposite the north entrance to Beihai Park, Xicheng District.

客家菜　西城区北海公园北门对面

Tel (010) 64042259

11am—2pm, 5pm—10pm. This pretty restaurant decorated completely in wood, on the edge of Qianhai Lake serves dishes from the Hakka ethnic minority, who originate from the South of China. Hakka food is simple and its ingredients very fresh: try the prawn kebabs in salt and the famous fish wrapped in paper. Often jam-packed.

Kao Rou Ji ⑦

Map III, C1

14 Qianhai Dongyan, Xicheng District.

烤肉季　西城区前海东沿 14 号

Tel (010) 64042554

11am—11pm. The Kao Rou Ji, Xinjiang restaurant, has been around since the Qing Dynasty. Ideally situated in the Lake Area, a couple of steps from the delightful Silver Ingot Bridge, it serves tasty lamb based food. Specialities not to miss are lamb with coriander and small sesame seed rolls.

▶ *From 50 to 100 yuan*

South Silk Road ㉔

Map III, C2

19 Shichahai Qianhai Xiyan, Xicheng District.

茶马古道　西城区前海西沿什刹海 19 号

Tel (010) 66155515

On the shores of Qianhai lake, in "Lotus Lane" restaurants line up and begin to resemble one another. This completely transparent space dreamed up by the painter Fang Lijun hits home. Delicious food from Yunnan and a pleasant terrace on fine days. It should be noted, for in Beijing there are not many terraces and to sit on the shores of the lake watching the pedalos (or skaters in winter) makes a worthwhile stop after a walk around the surrounding *hutong*. Try the lemon chicken, Kunming style aubergine, minted leaks and mushroom specialities, all drizzled with a fresh pear juice or home-made rice wine.

Pass By Bar ⑮

Map III, C2

108 Nan Luogu Xiang, Dongcheng District.

过客酒吧　东城区南锣鼓巷 108 号

Tel (010) 84038004

10am—2am. A couple of steps from the Songyuan Hotel, in the area around the Drum Tower, a small bar-restaurant set in a *siheyuan* opened by two oddballs, Xiaobian and Haiyan. There are photos on the walls, including several copies of National Geographic. A musical ambiance which goes from Indian pop to Zebda creates the atmosphere in this friendly and unusual bar. You must try the home-made mozzarella and the specialities of the house: the lamb kebab and Hutong Pizza.

Kong Yiji ⑨

Map III, B1

South bank of Shichahai, Deshengmennei Dajie, Xicheng District

孔乙己　西城区德胜门内大街什刹海南岸

Tel (010) 66184915/66184917

10am—2pm, 4:30pm—10:30pm. Named after the eponymous hero of the novel by Lu Xun, this very popular restaurant serves delicious Shaoxing food. It is ideally located on the bank of Shichahai, behind a white wall at the back of a small courtyard. Try the broad beans in aniseed, "drunken" shrimps, lamb browned with onions and sautéed noodles.

Café Sambal ③

Map III, C1

43 Doufuchi Hutong, Jiugulou Dajie, Xicheng District.

西城区旧鼓楼大街豆腐池胡同 43 号

Tel (010) 64004875

11am—midnight. A small up-to-date restaurant in the area of the Drum Tower, indicated by a red lantern on Jiugulou, difficult to find, but well worth it. Delicious Nyonya food (the Nyonya are Malaysian Chinese) served in a small house in a pleasant tastefully renovated courtyard. The tastiest dishes are deep fried chicken, chicken nyonya, satay, and fried long bean (mile long referring to their exceptional length) in a cashew nut sauce...Don't miss the dessert-banana boiled in coconut milk and pearls of cassava!

Nuage ⑭

Map III, C1

22 Qianhai Dongyan, Xicheng District.

庆云楼　西城区前海东沿 22 号

Tel (010) 64019581

11am—2pm, 5:30pm—10pm. One of the prettiest views in Beijing from this Vietnamese restaurant on the bank of the lakes, near to the Silver Ingot Bridge in a lovely big with many floors house. As pleasant by day as by night, this restaurant is well appreciated by expats and tourists: best reserve a little in advance. In the basement, the Club Nuage opened at the end of 2004; it is yet to conquer the Beijing night owls, but is still a pleasant place to have a drink in a musical atmosphere.

▶ *From 100 to 200 yuan*

Noble Restaurant ⑬

Map III, B1

Bajiao Ting (in Houhai Park, on the shores of the lake), Shiqiao dong, Deshengmennei Dajie, Xicheng District.

茶家傅茶馆　西城区德胜门内大街石桥洞八角亭 (后海公园内后海南岸)

Tel (010) 66160725/66166343

11am—midnight. On the banks of Houhai, near to the Kong Yiji restaurant, nestled in a still calm corner, beautiful glass and wood architecture houses a family cooking restaurant. A delight! Single menu at 150 yuan. Reservation only.

Zhang Qun Jia ㉓

Map III, C1

5 Yandai Xiejie, Houhai, Xicheng District.

张群家　西城区烟袋斜街 5 号

Tel (010) 84046662/13001176908 (Mobile)

A secret location at the heart of the very touristy Lake Area. No sign, so nothing to indicate where this tiny restaurant is, apart from the 3 steps which lead from the street to the old wood door. But is it a restaurant? It's actually one room where at most 6 people can sit, tastefully and simply decorated. First opened by Zhang Qun, a Chinese TV journalist to receive friends. Their passion led bit by bit to a larger circle of privileged few. His friend Qiang Lan, in the kitchen, prepares fresh and tasty Zhejiang and Suzhou food. Single menu at 150 yuan. Reservation only, at least 1 or 2 days in advance.

The Source ⑳

Map III, D2

14 Banchang Hutong (next to Lu Song Yuan Hotel), Nanluoguxiang, Kuanjie, Dongcheng District.

都江源　东城区南锣鼓巷宽街板厂胡同 14 号（位于侣松园宾馆旁）

Tel (010) 64003736

11am—2pm, 5pm—11pm. A Sichuan restaurant in a *siheyuan*: dinner is served in the courtyard when weather permits. Prettily decorated and delicious food. Single menu at 150 yuan. Booking compulsory.

▶ More than 200 yuan

Mei Fu ⑫

Map III, B1

24 Daxiangfeng Hutong, south bank of Houhai Lake, Xicheng District.

梅府　西城区后海南沿大翔凤胡同 24 号

Tel (010) 66126847

11:30am—2:30pm, 5:30pm—10:30pm. As much a treat to look at as a palace, Mei Fu is located within a traditional square courtyard house, in the midst of the *hutong*, decorated like a 1930's Shanghai boudoir. A team of young chefs prepare delicious Shanghai food, initially created by the Peking Opera star Mei Lanfang. The dishes are fresh and light, so that the famous singer kept his figure and his voice. Prices are high but this mildly confidential restaurant is considered by some as the best in the city.

Li Family Imperial Cuisine ⑩

Map III, B1

11 Yangfang Hutong, Deshengmennei Dajie, Xicheng District.

厉家菜　西城区德胜门内大街羊房胡同 11 号

Tel (010) 66180107

4:30pm—10pm. Mr Li's exclusive restaurant is hidden in a traditional courtyard house in the Lake Area. Here is served delicious and creative Imperial food. This restaurant has a high reputation and is frequented by expats. Reservation only and open only in evenings. A little difficult to find: call the restaurant or your hotel reception to give the taxi driver directions.

Sanlitun and Chaoyang District

▶ From 50 to 100 yuan

Bellagio ③

Map IV, B2

6 Gongti Xilu, Chaoyang District.
鹿港小镇　朝阳区工体西路 6 号
Tel (010) 65513533

11am—4am. As its name does not suggest, Bellagio is a Taiwanese restaurant. It is one of a chain, a little chic and well prized by the switched-on youth. Light food, using many herbs and ginger, and impressive ice creams.

Three Guizhou Men ⑧

Map IV, B2

West gate of the Workers' Stadium (above Coco Banana), Chaoyang District.
三个贵州人　朝阳区工人体育场西门
Tel (010) 58690598

10:30am—10:30pm. A Guizhou speciality restaurant inside the Workers' Stadium. Delicious food: try the special fondue (quite spicy!), sour fish soup or mint salad.

▶ From 100 to 200 yuan

Hatsune ⑤

Map IV, C3

2nd Floor of the Heqiao Building C, 8 Guanghua Lu, Chaoyang District.

隐泉日本料理　朝阳区光华路 8 号和乔大厦 C 座三层
Tel (010) 65813939

11:30am—2pm, 5:30pm—10pm. A Japanese restaurant located in the Central Business District. Modern decoration and very creative food: the rolls menu is astonishing; in particular try *the* Beijing duck roll.

Beijing Dadong Roast Duck Restaurant ②

Map IV, C2

Building 3, Tuanjiehu Beikou, Dongsanhuan, southeast corner of Changhong Qiao, Chaoyang District.

北京大董烤鸭店　朝阳区东三环长虹桥东南角团结湖北口 3 号楼
Tel (010) 65822892/65824003

11am—10pm. One of the best roast ducks in the city. This restaurant is very popular with the expats from the nearby Embassy Quarter, just as it is for Beijingers. Reservation strongly recommended.

The Le Quai ⑥

Map IV, B2

Gate 12 of the Workers' Stadium, Chaoyang District.

有璟阁　朝阳区工人体育场 12 号门
Tel (010) 65511636

11:30am—10pm. 250-year-old wooden house, re-located from Jiangsu Province to the Workers' Stadium. Good Chinese food, with Sichuan specialities. Lovely terrace. Booking advised.

Pure Lotus Vegetarian ⑦

Map IV, C2

In Zhongguo Wenlianyuan, 10 Nongzhanguan Nanlu, Chaoyang District.

净心莲素食餐厅 朝阳区农展馆南路 10 号中国文联院内

Tel (010) 65923627

9:30am—10pm. A creative vegetarian restaurant run by monks. Dishes with "amusing" names: No Birth no Death, Imperial Kitchen Buddha Jumps Over the Wall or even Yoga Salad… A bit hard to find, but well worth it! No smoking. Menus in English.

Assaggi ①

Map IV,B1

1 Sanlitun Beixiaojie, Sanlitun, Chaoyang District.

朝阳区 三里屯北小街 1 号

Tel (010) 84544508

11:30am—2:30pm, 5:30pm—11pm. An Italian restaurant in the Embassy Quarter. Pleasant and reasonably good food. Fixed price menus at midday with attractive prices (around 60 yuan).

▶ *Over 200 yuan*

Green Tea House ④

Map IV, B2

6 Gongti Xilu, Chaoyang District.

紫云轩 朝阳区工体西路 6 号

Tel (010) 65528310/65528311

10:30am—2:30pm, 6pm to midnight. Close to the French Cultural Centre. One of the switched-on and stylish places in the capital, very "New China", kept by two artist sisters and frequented by a mainly foreign clientele. The grandiose and refined decoration is worth the detour, and the food spectacularly produced is very creative. Prices are quite high, but you can also just go for a tea (around 100 yuan). Booking advised.

Around Dongzhimen

▶ *Less than 50 yuan*

Gui Jie ⑤

Map III, D1

Dongzhimennei Dajie, Dongcheng District.

簋街 东城区东直门大街

"Ghost Street", easily identified by its line of red lanterns, occupies the big thoroughfare of Dongzhimen: dozens of restaurants serve cheap and satisfying food all night long! It is a very popular place.

▶ *From 50 to 100 yuan*

Hua Jia Yi Yuan ⑥

Map III, D1

99 Dongzhimennei Dajie, Dongcheng District.

花家怡园 东城区东直门内大街 99 号

Tel (010) 64030677

A real institution in "Ghost Street", this very popular Beijing food restaurant set up in a big traditional house with several square courtyards. The main room is noisy and very lively, but you can ask to be put in the courtyard at the back. Good Beijing specialities. Book in advance or suffer having to queue for a good half hour!

Beijing Gong ①

Map III,E2

130 Chaoyangmennei Dajie, Chaoyang District.

北京宫正味大酒楼　朝阳区朝阳门内大街 130 号

Tel (010) 65236320

11am—2pm, 5pm—9:30pm. Very prettily decorated, this restaurant on Chaoyangmennei Dajie serves good Peking food at reasonable prices. The roast duck is a particular success.

▶ *From 100 to 200 yuan*

Café de la Poste ②

Map III, D1

58 Yonghegong Dajie, Dongcheng District.

东城区雍和宫大街 58 号

Tel (010) 64027047

www.cafedelapostecom.cn

9:30am—late. Closed Mon. The meeting place for the French community in Beijing, a couple of paces from the Lama Temple. Good bistro style food, wine list (the owner's vintage). To ease a sudden urge for steak and chips and chocolate mousse!

South of Qianmen

▶ *Less than 50 yuan*

Liqun Roast Duck Restaurant ⑪

Map III, C4

11 Beixiangfeng, Zhengyi Lu, northeast of Qianmen, Dongcheng District.

利群烤鸭店　东城区前门东北街正义路北祥凤 11 号

Tel (010) 67055578

10am—1:30pm, 4:30pm—10pm. Hard to find (ask the locals the way, they will know what you're looking for, then follow their advice), this family restaurant doesn't make any pretences. Plywood tables and plastic serviettes set the decoration for this old traditional square courtyard house (some traces of panelling). It's unimportant: it's not for the building that people come here, but Mr Zhang's delicious duck, prepared according to the art. Crispy skin served in little pancakes with scallions and plum sauce, generous flesh, the remains made into a tasty soup, all for a modest price. Booking advised.

In the west of the city

▶ *From 100 to 200 yuan*

Quanjude ⑯
Map III, B4
32 Qianmen Xidajie, Chongwen District.
全聚德烤鸭店　崇文区前门西大街 32 号
Tel (010) 65112418
11am—1:30pm, 4:30pm—8pm. Also at 9 Shuaifuyuan Hutong, Wangfujing Dajie, Dongcheng District.
全聚德烤鸭店　东城区王府井大街帅府园胡同 9 号
Tel (010) 65253310
11am—2pm, 4:30pm—9pm. The kingdom of Beijing duck since 1864! But helped by its fame, the Quanjude, which now has several outlets in Beijing, has become very touristy and quite dear. And true lovers of the

dish will tell you that the roast duck is maybe done better elsewhere!

Going out for a drink

Eatea Tea House
Map III, D1
23 Guozijian Jie, Dongcheng District.
留贤馆　东城区国子监街 28 号
Tel (010) 84048539
Opposite the Confucius Temple, in a very calm *hutong*, this tea house constitutes a restful stop where you can discover the tea ceremony. In glasses as small as thimbles, a woman in a traditional outfit serves you one of the best brews in China in several infusions (the second is considered the best, the one which gives off all the tea aromas) and explains the benefits.

Chajiafu Tea House

Map III, B1

South bank of Houhai Lake, Deshengmennei Dajie, Xicheng District.

茶家傅茶馆　西城区德胜门内大街后海南岸

Tel (010) 66160725/66166343/66571588

10:30am—midnight. This very calm tea house is attached to the neighbouring Noble Restaurant, in a quiet corner of the Lake Area. Large rooms for groups and small rooms looking out onto the lake. Tea ceremony.

In the Lake Area

Most pleasant cafés are located in the Lake Area and go for a "muddled" style, bringing together old pieces of wooden furniture, lively colours and atmospheric music.

The Drum & Bell

Map III, B1

41 Zhonglouwan Hutong, Dongcheng District.

东城区钟楼湾胡同 41 号

On a very pretty little square behind the Drum Tower, the Drum & Bell benefits from a pleasant roof terrace where you can admire the view over the old grey houses of the quarter whilst playing go and at the same time tasting lamb kebab.

Bai Feng Bar

Map III, C1

3 Qianhai Dongyan, Xicheng District.

白枫酒吧　西城区前海东沿 3 号

Tel (010) 64018541

11am—2am. When you see the multitude of noisy and colourful bars along the banks of Houhai, you'd find it hard to imagine it as one of the calmest quarters in Beijing a few years ago! The phenomenon was started by Bai Feng, owner of the neighbouring Nuage restaurant. This small bar with its charm inexplicably intact, is right on the edge of the lake. The green plants, the wooden furniture and the warm tones make this place somewhere for a privileged pause. Threatened with demolition for some time already (to widen the road along the lake), make sure you call before going there, to find out if it's still standing!

Here

Map III, C2

97 Nanluoguxiang, Dongcheng District.

东城区南锣鼓巷 97 号

Tel (010) 84014246

10am—midnight. Numerous bars on this street, where stands also the Conservatory of Dramatic Arts. Owned by a photographer, the Here is a den for students and adherents of the image (photo and cinema).

In the same spirit its charming neighbour **Xiaoxin** at No. 103.

Tel (010)64036956.

Waiting for Godot

Map III, D1

Building 4, Jiaodaokou Dongdajie, Dongcheng District.

等待戈多酒吧　东城区交道口东大街 4 号楼
Tel (021) 64073093

9:30am—1am. Very nice atmosphere in this bar which pays an improbable homage to Beckett. Café, Belgium beer, cocktails… to sip slumped in an armchair whilst looking through the selection of second-hand books, CDs and DVDs.

22 Film Café
Map III, B1
103 Deshengmennei Dajie, Xihai Dongyan, Xicheng District.
西城区西海东沿德胜门内大街 103 号
Tel (010) 84050094

1pm—midnight. On the banks of Xihai Lake, this cinema café was opened by film lovers, former students at the Beijing Film Academy. Movie posters adorn the walls and independent films shown on weekends.

Bed
Map III, C1
17 Zhangwang Hutong, Xicheng District.
西城区张旺胡同 17 号
Tel (010) 84001554

5pm—late. In a *hutong* off Jiugulou Dajie, behind the Drum Tower, hides one of the prettiest bars in Beijing. Run by Cho, the owner of Café Sambal (located in a parallel street), the Bed is decorated in minimalist style (smooth concrete, antiques and faded colours) and has Malaysian style tapas. It's in a traditional house consisting of several rooms with old furnishings and a square courtyard, which is very pleasant in summer.

In Sanlitun

Bar Blu
Map IV, B2
4th Floor of Tongli Studios, Sanlitun Beilu, Chaoyang District.
朝阳区三里屯北路同里工作室 4 楼
Tel (010) 64167567

11am—late. A bar bathed in blue light where you can drink good cocktails.

Aperitivo
Map IV, B2
43 Sanlitun Beilu, Chaoyang District.
朝阳区三里屯北路 43 号
Tel (010) 64177793

10am—late. A European style bar open late into the night which offers a choice of drinks and Italian food. Very well liked, this little place is never empty. Wi-Fi Internet access and Happy Hours.

In Chaoyang District

Music Bars

Here you'll find the alternative Beijing music scene. You can get gig guides in the free dailies *That's Beijing*, *Time Out*, *City Weekend*... distributed in the happening bars and restaurants in the Lake Area and in Sanlitun.

Lan

4th Floor of LG Twin Towers, 12T Jianguomenwai Dajie, Chaoyang District.
朝阳区建国门外大街 12T 号 LG 双子楼 4 层
Tel (010) 51096012

The darling of switched-on Beijing: a restaurant and bar conceived by Philippe Starck, in a completely baroque style. Jet-set atmosphere, drinks from 60 yuan.

Yugongyishan
Map IV, B2

1 Gongti Beilu, Chunxiu Lu entrance, in the car park, Chaoyang District.
愚公移山　朝阳区工体北路 1 号春秀路入口停车场
Tel (010) 64150687

A bar on the basement level of a car park, opposite the Workers' Stadium, in a New York loft style. Very good concert venue with a small room at the back with a billiard table. Extremely warm atmosphere.

Get Lucky Bar

500 metres to the east of the south entrance of the University of International Business and Economics, near Taiyanggong, Chaoyang District.
朝阳区太阳宫附近经贸大学南门往东 500 米
Tel (010) 64299109/64204249

2pm—2am. One of the first bars to have put on rock and Chinese punk with a very active programme of live concerts. The Get Lucky is always at the forefront of the alternative scene and has even opened a second venue, in Oriental Qicai World, close to Xingbalu Bar Street, Nüren Jie, Chaoyang District.

朝阳区女人街星吧路酒吧街东方七彩大世界

Tel (010) 84483335

11am—2am.

Nameless Highland

Building 14, Anhuili Area 1, Yayuncun, Chaoyang District.

朝阳区亚运村安慧里 1 区 14 号楼

Tel (010) 64891613

6pm—2am. Quite far from the centre, the Nameless Highland, with its large room on two floors, welcomes local groups with quality gigs.

What? Bar

Map III, C3

72 Beichang Jie, Xicheng District, north of the west gate of the Forbidden City.

西城区北长街 72 号故宫西门往北

7pm—midnight. A couple of steps from the Forbidden City, this tiny place makes the foundations of the thousand-year-old monuments shake with punk and rock concerts given by the loudest groups on the new Chinese scene. Drinks from 10 yuan.

Poachers Inn

Map IV, B2

43 Sanlitun Beilu, Chaoyang District.

朝阳区三里屯北路 43 号

Tel (010) 64172632

From 8pm. Student bar where all drinks are 10 yuan. This tariff explains this place's success. A crowd surges here every night to dance to the latest international hits.

Tango

Map III, D1

South gate of Ditan Park, near the Jindingxuan restaurant, Dongcheng District.

东城区地坛公园南门金鼎轩餐厅旁

Tel (010) 64002721

24/7. Opened in 2004, this night club is divided into three spaces: dance floor, lounge and music bar. International DJs.

Suzie Wong

Map IV, C2

Area 1 Nongzhanguan Lu, west gate of Chaoyang Park, Chaoyang District.

朝阳区农展馆路 1 号朝阳公园西门

Tel (010)65937889/65936049

From 7pm. Expats at the exit to Chaoyang Park, Suzie Wong recreates a 1930's Shanghai atmosphere. Pleasant terrace in the summer.

Rock'N'Roll

4, Gongti Beilu (behind The Loft), Chaoyang District.

朝阳区工体北路 4 号（在 The Loft 后面）

Tel (010) 65929856

8pm—5am. A typically Chinese nightclub: techno at the back, *go-go dancers* in the room at the back

Mix

Map IV, B2

North gate of the Workers' Stadium, Chaoyang District.

朝阳区工人体育场北门

Tel (010) 65302889

From 8pm. A pioneer among Beijing nightclubs. Always full to the brim, even during the week. Hip-hop music.

Vics

Map IV, B2

North gate of the Workers' Stadium, Chaoyang District.

朝阳区工人体育场北门

Tel (010) 65936215

From 8:30pm. Located opposite Mix, Vics has hardly been empty since opening several years ago. R&B, pop, soul, reggae, hip-hop.

Inner Affairs

6 Xiliujie, Sanlitun, Chaoyang District.

朝阳区三里屯西六街 6 号

Tel (010) 84540899

6:30pm—late. Nightclub in a more chic setting, in the Sanlitun office quarter. A gigantic golden Buddha dominates the dance floor where you get going to house music or techno.

Banana

Map IV, B4

Scitech Hotel, 22 Jianguomenwai Dajie, Chaoyang District.

朝阳区建国门外大街 22 号赛特饭店

Tel (010) 65283636

8:30pm—4am. A "factory" type disco: enormously global, efficient techno and international DJs. Chinese clientele.

Things to do

Guided tours of Beijing

To explore the city off the beaten track and walk in the footsteps of a Beijinger, get a student to accompany you who will show you his city in English: check announcements at the website of Beijing Foreign Studies University and those in the English weeklies given out free in the bars.

Sporting activities

Dongdan Indoor Swimming Pool

Dongdan Sports Centre, A2 Dahua Lu, Dongcheng District.

东单游泳馆　东城区大华路甲 2 号东单体育中心

Tel (010) 65231241

9am—10pm/30 yuan

A covered pool for those without one at the hotel (refreshing in the height of summer). Very well situated in the centre.

Climbing at Boulder Bar

(1st Floor), 1 Shengu Jiayuan, Anzhenqiao, Dongcheng District.

攀岩 Boulder 酒吧　东城区安贞桥胜古家园 1 号

Tel (010) 64441965

9am—midnight

A central Beijing bar, meeting place for all climbers, attracted by the climbing wall installed in the bar.

Argentine Tango

on the banks of Houhai, opposite the entrance to Beihai Park.

阿根廷探戈　后海沿岸北海公园入口对面

At nightfall, couples, young and less young, come to dance the tango on the banks of Houhai Lake. A strange vision of Chinese dancers moving about at dusk to the sounds of Carlos Gardel as the neon lights of the neighbouring bars are reflected in the dark waters of the Imperial lake.

Beijing Milun School of Traditional Kung Fu.

北京米伦功夫学校

Kung fu, Shaolin kung fu, *taichi* and *qigong* lessons are given in a traditional square courtyard near Wangfujing (*Map III, D3*) or in Ritan Park (*Map IV, B3*). Individual lessons (150 yuan) or groups (70 yuan). For information go to www.kungfuinchina.com.

Other Activies

Houhai, boating in summer, ice skating in winter on the imperial lakes.

Martial Arts Practice as well at dawn in the parks.

Hiking at the weekend, to the Great Wall or in the villages on the outskirts of Beijing. Contact the Beijing Hikers club which edits a guidebook: www.beijinghikers.com.

Cinema

Cherry Lane Movies

Map IV, C1

Kent Centre, Anjialou Jie (on Liangmaqiao Lu, a road off the corner of Gaolan Building), Chaoyang District.

朝阳区安家楼街肯特中心（亮马桥路高澜大厦拐角）

Tel (010) 64305318

www.cherrylanemovies.com.cn

50 yuan. Screenings of Chinese films of today and yesteryear, with English sub-titles. A programme is available on the website or in the English magazines *That's Beijing*, *City Weekend*, *Time Out*... Screenings start always at 8pm, and are preceded by a free buffet 7:30pm onwards.

Daguanlou

Map III, C4

36 Dashilan, Xuanwu District.

大观楼影城　宣武区大栅栏 36 号

Tel (010) 63030878

25—35 yuan. Popular cinema situated on Dashilan shopping street.

Xin Dong'an Cinema

Map III, D3

Xin Dong'an Plaza (5th Floor), 138 Wangfujing Dajie, Dongcheng District.

新东安影院　东城区王府井大街 138 号新东安大厦 5 层

Tel (010) 65281838

30—50 yuan. Modern and very central theatre, on the famous Wangfujing Dajie. For a chance to see the latest US blockbuster dubbed into Mandarin!

Massage

Bodhi

Map IV, B2

17 Gongti Beilu, Chaoyang District.

菩提按摩中心　朝阳区工体北路 17 号

Tel (010) 64179595

www.bodhi.com.cn

11am—3am. The most glamorous Beijing massage parlour is located right opposite the north entrance of the Workers' Stadium in Sanlitun. Chinese massage (foot massage and full body massage) and Thai massage (an old aromatherapy technique) given by professionals, manicure and pedicure services also available. Top quality services given in a relaxing setting simply decorated and refined, and accompanied by delicate thoughtfulness: warm towels on the neck, fresh fruit juice and healthy snacks offered... English spoken at reception. From 138 yuan. Promotions from Mon to Thurs before 5pm, 78 yuan.

Beijing Miaoshou Foot Massage
Map III, D3

Gangmei Building (6th Floor), 1 Xiagongfu, Wangfujing Dajie, Dongcheng District.

北京妙手足疗会馆　东城区王府井大街霞公府街 1 号港美大厦 6 层

Tel (010) 6512086

Noon—1am. Very well placed, near the Wangfujing crossroads, and easily reached (behind the Beijing Hotel), this salon specialises in foot massage (88 yuan for 80 minutes) and also offers a traditional body massage (118 yuan for 1 hour) and manicure/pedicure service.

Dragonfly
Map III, D3

60 Donghuamen Dajie, Dongcheng District.

悠庭保健会所　东城区东华门大街 60 号

Tel (010) 65279368

This chain of chic salons offers foot massage, shiatsu and Chinese massage from 120 yuan/hour. Very well situated, near the entrance to the Forbidden City.

Shows

▶ *Peking Opera*

Lao She Tea House
Map III, C4

3 Qianmen Xidajie, Xuanwu District.

老舍茶馆　宣武区前门西大街 3 号

Tel (010) 63036830

www.laosheteahouse.com

9:30am—10pm. A couple of steps from the well-known pedestrian street of Dashilan, the Lao She Tea House presents in its ancient setting, various traditional theatrical forms: Peking opera, puppet or magic shows, acrobatics, storytelling... Mixed spectacle for the general public, every day at 7:50pm; duration: 90 minutes. Booking required. Tickets from 180 to 380 yuan. At the weekend from 3pm to 4:30pm, excerpts from Peking opera only. Tickets from 30 to 90 yuan.

Chang'an Grand Theatre

Map IV, A3

7 Jianguomennei Dajie, Dongcheng District.

长安大戏院　东城区建国门内大街 7 号

Tel (010) 65101310

A modern theatre well placed in the centre of Beijing. Excerpts from traditional opera every day at 7:30pm. Duration: 2 hours. Tickets from 50 to 800 yuan.

▶ Puppets

China Puppet Theatre

Area 1 Anhua Xili, Beisanhuan Zhonglu, Chaoyang District.

中国木偶剧院　朝阳区北三环中路安华西里 1 区

Tel (010) 64229487

Simplicity and charm of Chinese shadow puppets. Telephone ahead for the programme.

▶ Martial arts

The Red Theatre

44 Xingfu Dajie, Chongwen District.

北京红剧场　崇文区幸福大街 44 号

Tel (010) 67142473

"The Legend of Kung Fu" show every day at 7:30pm: spotlights aimed at young boys dressed in garish costumes, plot full of pathos, special effects…

▶ Acrobats

Chaoyang Theatre

Map IV, C3

36 Sanhuan Beilu, Chaoyang District.

朝阳剧场　朝阳区三环北路 36 号

Tel (010) 51664511

Kitsch circus performers and contortionists in a theatre where tourists flock, on the edge of the 3rd Ring Road. Every day at 7:15pm. Tickets cost from 180 to 680 yuan.

Tianqiao Acrobatics
95 Tianqiaoshichang Lu, to the east of Beiwei Lu, Xuanwu District.
天桥剧场　宣武区北纬路东天桥市场路 95 号
Tel (010) 65231455
Less well-known and less flashy than the Chaoyang Theatre. Two shows per day, every day 5:30pm to 6:30pm and 7:15pm to 8:40pm. Tickets cost 180 to 380 yuan.

▶ *Theatre and dance*

Capital Theatre
Map III, D3
22 Wangfujing Dajie, Dongcheng District.
首都剧场　东城区王府井大街 22 号
Tel (010) 65249847
The most renowned theatre in Beijing, located in the centre on Wangfujing, is also the seat of the prestigious National Theatre Troup of China. Classical performances with obvious stylization.

People's Art Experimental Theatre
3rd Floor of the Capital Theatre, 22 Wangfujing Dajie, Dongcheng District.
人民艺术剧院实验剧场　东城区王府井大街 22 号首都剧场 3 层
Tel (010) 65263338
Very visual shows by young Chinese directors. Performance at 7:30pm.

National Theatre
Map III, B4
West of Tian'anmen Square.
国家大剧院，天安门广场西侧
Conceived by the French architect Paul Andreu and inaugurated in 2007, it welcomes large scale local and foreign productions.

Popular shows

▶ *Bird market*

Huawei Nanlu, Chaoyang District (to the south of Panjiayuan Antiques Market).
鸟市　朝阳区华为南路（潘家园市场南面）
The bird market opens its doors at 10am. At weekends an extra

performance at 3pm, wrestlers, storytellers, sword swallowers, Dragon dance performances…
In the midst of a noisy and mixed crowd, don't forget this show because popular arts are disappearing!

Shopping

If you are particularly interested in a shop or stand in the middle of a market, ask for a business card or the mobile phone number of the owner so you can find it again.

▶ *Markets*

Panjiayuan Antiques Market
Map I, E4
Panjiayuan Qiao, Dongsanhuan Nanlu, Chaoyang District.
潘家园旧货市场　朝阳区东三环南路潘家园桥
Tel (010) 67752405

Mon.—Fri.: 8:30am—6pm, weekend: 4:30am—6pm. Not to be missed! Everything is here under the huge extremely lively roofs at this flea market: crafts, ethnic clothes and jewellery, antiques, china, Chinese furniture, sculpture, Tintin books in Chinese...

Beijing Antique City
Map I, E3
21 Dongsanhuan Nanlu, Chaoyang District.
北京古玩城 朝阳区东三环南路 21 号
Tel (010) 67747711/67736018
9:30am—6:30pm. A couple of feet away from the antiques market, this modern building sells—with no atmosphere—the same type of goods.

can also have clothes made to measure. Haggling is possible.

Yaxiu Market

Map IV, B2

58 Gongti Beilu, Chaoyang District.

雅秀市场　朝阳区工体北路 58 号

Tel (010) 64151726

9am—9:30pm. In Sanlitun, altogether 4 levels. Clothes, tailoring, crafts, curios, leather goods, shoes… A very practical place to buy all your souvenirs. Prices aren't fixed so you could haggle. Avoid it if you don't like crowds: tourists arrive by the busload!

Silk Market

Map IV, B3

1 Xiushui Jie, Jianguomenwai Dajie, Chaoyang District.

秀水街　朝阳区建国门外大街秀水街 1 号

9am—7pm. The famous Silk Lanes was transformed into a modern building a few feet from where it used to stand, on Jianguomenwai Dajie. Clothes and crafts. You

Hongqiao Market
Map I, D3

46 Tiantan Donglu, Chongwen District, near to the Temple of Heaven.

红桥市场　崇文区天坛东路 46 号天坛附近

Tel (010) 67133354

8:30am—7pm. A popular market where you can find a bit of everything: electronics and costume jewellery on the ground floor, textiles on the first, and the "pearl market" on the second floor.

Nüren Jie Flower Market
Map I, E2

Hua Jie, 9 Maizidian Xilu, Chaoyang District, Northeast of the Kempinski Hotel.

女人街花市　朝阳区麦子店西路 9 号花街凯宾斯基酒店西北

Tel (010) 64636145

9am—6pm (6:30pm on weekends). At the "Ladies Street" Flower Market, under large greenhouses, you can find orchids year round, Chinese peonies in April, heady perfumed tuberose... Shops selling crockery in the basement.

▶ *Shopping streets*

Friendship Store
Map IV, B3

17 Jianguomenwai Dajie, Chaoyang District.

友谊商店　朝阳区建国门外大街 17 号

Tel (010) 65003311

9:30am—8:30pm. A real institution, and even if it has lost much of its interest, it's still a good place for quality cashmere. Ideal for tourists in a hurry because you can find a whole pile of souvenirs and craft items (prices at top end). There's also a supermarket, a bakery and a bookshop selling foreign newspapers and books about China in English.

Dashilan
Map III, C4

South of Tian'anmen Square.

大栅栏　天安门广场南面

9am—5pm. It's also called the "Wangfujing" of the Qing

Dynasty. Go there for the famous Chinese traditional medicine shop Tong Ren Tang (No.24), the oldest material shop in the city, tea shops as well as the very lively atmosphere.

Liulichang

Map III, B4

琉璃厂

9am—5pm. Wrongly called "Antique Street", it's the chance for a picturesque stroll. You will find here above all prints, pretty rice papers and everything to do with calligraphy.

China World Trade Centre

Map IV, B3

1 Jianguomenwai Dajie, Chaoyang District.

国贸中心　朝阳区建国门外大街 1 号

Tel (010) 65052288

10am—9pm. Next to China World Hotel, several floors of malls lined with luxury fashion boutiques.

Wangfujing Dajie

Map III, D3

王府井大街

For seven centuries a large commercial thoroughfare which never ceases to modernise itself and adapt to the times. Large American style malls, huge hoardings of international

brands...Some shops not to be missed: **Shengxifu** hat shop, at No. 196, where you can find a real Mao cap; specialist in traditional shoes **Tongshenghe**, at No. 225; the material shop **Beijing Silk Store**, at No.194, where you can find a wide choice of cashmere and silk.

Gaobeidian

Map I, E3

Chaoyang District.

高碑店　朝阳区

Recently set up on the edge of Chaoyang District, it is nicknamed "Antiques Village". In reality what you find are some quite expensive antiques, but above all reproductions and the factory outlets of those capable of making classical Chinese furniture, adapting them to your tastes.

▶ *Fashion*

Ritan Office Building

Map IV, B3

15 Guanghua Lu, south gate of Ritan Park, Chaoyang District.

日坛商务楼　朝阳区日坛公园南门光华路 15 号

Tel (010) 85619556

9am—9pm. An old office building reinvested by shops selling sharp inexpensive fashion. The place is well appreciated by switched-on Beijingers. A good location for cashmere on the ground floor. On the right in the corridor.

Dongsi Dajie

Numerous shops on **Dongsi** Dajie. Ready wear fashion, shoes, wedding dresses...

Nali Mall

Map IV, B2

Sanlitun Beijie, Chaoyang District.

朝阳区三里屯北街

Tel (010) 64132663

10am—8pm. Recently set up in Sanlitun (close to Yaxiu Market), it's a dead end off the famous "Bar Street" where you can find a row of fashion shops and restaurants. Small piles of silk, shoes, dresses, costume, jewellery, leather goods…

▶ Outdoor equipment store

23 Dongsanhuan Lu, Chaoyang District, close to the Jingguang Centre tower.

户外用品商店 朝阳区东三环路 23 号京广中心附近

Tel (010) 65859312

9am—5pm. Masses of interesting goods in this army surplus store located on the East 3rd Ring Road: boots (between 10 and 200 yuan), camouflage kit (70 to 90 yuan), very warm khaki army coats, very useful in winter (520 yuan), badges (from 2 to 8 yuan)… very hardwearing lovely bags for the return journey at 25 yuan. If you go on expedition: khaki duvets (100 yuan), camp beds, sleeping bags, magnifiers, compasses, binoculars…

▶ Handicraft

Map IV, B2

Tongli Studios, Sanlitun Beilu (Bar street), Chaoyang District.

同里工作室 朝阳区三里屯北路(酒吧街)

Tel (010) 64176668

In Sanlitun. Everything for the house: candles, lamps, crockery…

Spin

6 Fangyuan Xilu, Chaoyang District (next to the Lido Hotel).

朝阳区芳园西路 6 号（丽都饭店旁）

Tel (010) 64378649

11am—9:30pm. Very nice porcelain Jingdezhen crockery, created by Chinese designers.

▶ Bookshops

Wangfujing Foreign Languages Bookstore

Map III, D3

235 Wangfujing Dajie, Dongcheng District.

外文书店 东城区王府井大街 235 号

Tel (010) 65126903

9am—9pm. You can find here maps of Beijing, books in English on history and Chinese culture, language learning methods…

Timezone 8

Map I, E1

Dashanzi 798 Art District, 4 Jiuxianqiao Lu, Chaoyang District.

东八时区艺术书屋 朝阳区酒仙桥路 4 号大山子 798 艺术区

Tel (010) 84560336

The best contemporary art bookshop opened by the American Robert Bernell. Good selection of contemporary Chinese art, latest international reviews, beautiful books on artists to be reckoned with or others less well known…

British Council China Beijing

4th floor Area 1, Liangmahe Office Building, 8 Dongsanhuan Beilu, Chaoyang District.

英国驻华大使馆文化教育处　朝阳区东
三环北路 8 号亮马河办公楼 1 座 4 层
Tel (010) 65906903
www. britishcouncil.org

French Cultural Centre

18 Gongti Xilu, Chaoyang District.
法国文化中心　朝阳区工体西路 18 号
Tel (010) 65535482
www. ccfpekin.org

▶ *Photography*

Beijing Photographic Equipment City

4 Wukesong Lu, Haidian District.
北京摄影器材城　海淀区五棵松路 4 号
Tel (010) 88119797
9am—6pm. Far from the centre and difficult to find, this place will delight the most motivated photographers. For rock bottom prices, a wide choice of equipment: old SLR cameras or the latest models, video cameras... To be negotiated, of course.

Xiangshenghang

Map III, D3

22 Meishuguan Dajie, Dongcheng District.
祥生行　东城区美术馆大街 22 号
Tel (010) 84034138
8:30am—7pm. Close to the Fine Arts Museum, in the centre, a very professional photo lab. Film developing for 25 to 45 yuan. Wide choice of photo equipment.

▶ *Electronics*

Haidian District, where most of the universities are situated, is also endowed with electronics and IT business.

Hailong Shopping Mall

1 Zhongguancun Dajie, Haidian District.
海龙电子大厦　海淀区中关村大街 1 号
Tel (010) 82663838
9am—5:30pm. A five-storey building where all the top names in IT are represented. Wide choice of MP3 players, DVD players, Hi-Fi separates, games, software... The equipment is the same as in Europe, but prices are often much keener: haggling allowed.

For the same type of thing, see also the **Taipingyang** Computer Market, 52 Haidian Lu, Haidian District (*Map I, B1*). 9am—5:30pm.

Zhonghai Computer Market

27 Haidian Lu, Haidian District.
中海电脑城　海淀区海淀路 27 号
Tel (010) 82615921
9am—5:30pm. Second-hand computer equipment (keyboards, hard disks...) at very low prices.

▶ *Paper, calligraphy material*

In the shops on **Wusi Road**, opposite the Fine Arts Museum (*Map III, D3*), you can find calligraphy material, very good paper, exercise books of all sizes. Customers consist mainly

of students of plastic arts. You can also obtain other identical products (paint boxes, sculpture material, felt pens for graphic artists, architects pens...) at very favourable prices.

Calligraphy material and very good quality paper all along Liulichang (琉璃厂) (*Map III, B4*).

▶ *Traditional toys*

Kite, a kind of traditional Chinese toys, in the shops in the road by the **Lama Temple** (雍和宫) (*Map III, D1*).

▶ *Tea*

Pretty tea shops/houses in **Dashilan**(大栅栏) (*Map III, C4*).

Tian Fu

Map III, D3

Danyao Dasha, Wangfujing Dajie, Dongcheng District.

天福茗茶　东城区王府井大街丹耀大厦

Tel (010) 65240958

9am—11pm. The Tian Fu's Tea chain has many stores in Beijing, of which this one is well located on Wangfujing. Numerous tea varieties, whose price depends on the "blend" and the quality. Tastings on site.

To takeaway: flowers for infusion, sweets flavoured with green tea (nougats, biscuits...), pistachios fragranced with roses.

▶ *Material*

To take home in your cases, silk, cashmere, pretty ethnic prints... Or made-to-measure clothes, curtains, cushions...

Daxin Textile Store

253 Chaoyangmennei Dajie, at the crossing of Dongsi Dajie, Chaoyang District.

大新纺织品商店　朝阳区东四大街岔路口朝阳门内大街 253 号

Tel (010) 84023919

A large variety of materials, cashmere and silks of every colour. A stall at the entrance to the shop offers a wide choice of Blue Nanjing cloths and multi-coloured ethnic cloth. Discounts on remnants on the 1st floor: very low priced velvet, cotton and kitsch prints. Tailoring service available.

Beijing Silk Store

Map III, D3

194 Wangfujing Dajie, Dongcheng District.

北京丝织品商店　东城区王府井大街 194 号

9am—9pm. More expensive than the previous store, due to its

tourist location.

Tailoring service. Very beautiful silks. A stall at the rear of the shop offers original textiles such as lacquered or wild silks. Large choice of cashmere is also available, as well as scarves, dressing gowns and other ready made clothes if you don't have time to visit the tailor (prices a little higher).

Beijing art

As Beijing rushes towards modernisation, cultural offerings become more colourful. Moreover, the capital is a true cultural laboratory, cradle of contemporary avantgardists of plastic arts, cinema or music. But this artistic life often reveals itself outside of the museums and other official places, sometimes even out of the city itself. To find exhibitions and performances, check out the English newspapers *That's Beijing*, *City Weekend*, *Time Out*… given out in hotels, bars and restaurants.

▶ *Museums*

National Art Museum of China
Map III, D2
1 Wusi Dajie, Dongcheng District.
中国美术馆　东城区五四大街 1 号
Tel (010) 64012252
www.namoc.org
9am—4pm. 20 yuan. The Art Museum organises large national and international exhibitions, like that of the selection of Impressionist paintings from the Orsay Gallery in Paris held in 2005 on the occasion of the Year Of France in China (The crowds were such that the museum stayed open all night following the final day!). In 1979 the museum entered into the history of contemporary art when the "7 stars" avant-garde group roughly attached their work to the railings: this anti-establishment act turned the place into a symbol of a culture stifled by the weight of the institution. Warning: closes at 4pm!

China Millennium Monument Art Museum
Map II, A2
9 Fuxing Lu, Haidian District.
中华世纪坛艺术博物馆　海淀区复兴路 9 号
Tel (010) 59802222
www.bj2000.org.cn
9am—6pm. 30 yuan. The gigantic and gleaming Millennium Museum is divided into 4 parts: art of the Orient, Western art, multimedia and digital art and modern art. Large quality exhibitions each year.

▶ *Exhibition*

Confucius Institute Headquarters
Block A, Desheng Up-town, No.129, Deshengmenwai Dajie
孔子学院总部　北京市西城区德胜门外大街 129 号德胜尚城 A 座
www.hanban.org.
Welcome to China Exploratorium(中国文化体验中心).

▶ *Art galleries*

Courtyard Gallery

Map III, C3

95 Donghuamen Dajie, Dongcheng District.

四合苑画廊　东城区东华门大街 95 号

Tel (010) 65268882

www.courtyard-gallery.com

Tues. to Sun.. 11am—6pm. Situated a few feet from the east gate of the Forbidden City, at the heart of the historical centre, the Courtyard (in the basement, under the Courtyard Restaurant which is part of the same establishment) is one of China's pioneering galleries in the field of contemporary art. Ideal for finding China's artistic scene.

Red Gate Gallery

Dongbianmen Jiaolou, Chongwenmen, Chongwen District.

红门画廊　崇文区崇文门东便门角楼

Tel (010) 65251005

www.redgategallery.com

9am—5pm. Set in an old observation tower, the Red Gate also stands out as a pioneer: it was inaugurated by Brian Wallace in 1991. This Australian studied art in Beijing in the 1980's and continues to explore the avant-garde scene in search of new talent.

Creation Gallery

North of Ritan Donglu, near Ritan Park, Chaoyang District.

可创铭佳艺苑　朝阳区日坛东路北面

Tel (010) 85617570

10am—7pm. Run by a descendant of the calligrapher Li Keran, this gallery shows classical Chinese works.

Dashanzi 798 Art Factory

Map I, E1

4 Jiuxianqiao Lu, Dashanzi Art District, Chaoyang District.

大山子 798 艺术工厂　朝阳区大山子艺术区酒仙桥路 4 号

About 11am—7pm. This is the most impressive of places dedicated to contemporary art. Originally an old industrial complex situated on the outskirts of Beijing on the airport road. Galleries and artists workshops (as well as restaurants, shops, cafés and bars) have been here since 2002. Thus these electrical component factories, the jewel of China's industry in the time of Mao, built in 1957 by architects from East Germany in a Bauhaus inspired style, have become in a few years one of the most dynamic artist communities in China, a real urban and artistic phenomenon (places of this kind have appeared elsewhere in China). A part of the factories is still active and this is what makes this place original. But this place is threatened with demolition by real estate developers who have their eyes on its privileged location.

Some galleries at Dashanzi 798:

798 Space
Tel (010) 64384862
www.798space.com
11am—11pm. photos and paintings of already renowned artists.

798 Photo Gallery
Tel (010) 64381784
www.798photogallery.cn
10am—6pm. A gallery exclusively dedicated to photography.

Beijing Tokyo Art Projects
北京东京艺术工程
Tel (010)84573245
www.tokyo-gallery.com
10:30am—6:30pm. Closed Mon. One of Dashanzi's pioneers.

Chinese Contemporary Beijing
北京中国当代画廊
Tel (010) 84562421
www.chinesecontemporary.com

11am—7pm. Often monumental works of art (sculptures) are exhibited in this gallery with very high roof.

Thinking Hands
思想手工作室
The office of the gallery of Huang Rui and Bérénice Angremy, the organizers of DIAF, is the lungs of the community. Festival posters and brochures are on sale here...

Xin Dong Cheng Gallery
程东昕国际当代艺术空间
Tel (010)643354579
10am—5pm. The biggest names in Chinese art are exhibited here.

At Café
爱特咖啡
The meeting place of the switched-on bohemian set: snacks, drinks, in a pretty modern setting; and "THE" bookshop of contemporary art in China.

Timezone 8
东八时区艺术书屋
Other lesser known artists' villages exist on the outskirts of Beijing. They are difficult to find: ask at hotel reception for their location then explain the way to the taxi driver.

Caochangdi
5 kilometres north of Dashanzi, Chaoyang District (on the Airport road, take the exit after Wuhuan Lu, and then the first right; turn to take the road opposite the Chang Jian driving school).
草场地　朝阳区大山子以北 5 公里

This village is Dashanzi's little brother, but less commercial: many artists have quit 798 to set up here. See the **Platform China** gallery, as well as the annex to the **Courtyard Gallery and China Art Archives and Warehouse.**

Liquor Factory, 10 minutes driving north of Dashanzi, Chaoyang District (take the Jingcheng Expressway to the Wangjing Kejiyuan exit, turn west then take Lize Xijie; drive for 10 kilometres as far as Beihuqu). Created in 2005, this village brings together thirty or so galleries and artists workshops (those of Zhang Xiaogang and Zeng Hao). See the **Arario** Korean gallery.

Songzhuang Artist's Village, by the Jingcheng Expressway as far as the Xima Zhuang exit; drive as far as the Beiguan roundabout, then take the Jingha Expressway as far as Ren Zhuan; three sets of traffic lights further on is the entrance, close to a petrol station. The first artist's village in Beijing was formed ten years or so ago. It housed the biggest studios: Fang Lijun, Yue Minjun, and Wang Qingsong... The village institution, **Artist's Village Gallery**, organises festivals in summer and offers visits: 1 day, 100 yuan/person. transport and meal included

Tel (010) 69598343.

History

Beiing, which literally means "Northern Capital", used to be known as Peking. It is not only one of the most populated cities in the world, but also one of the oldest inhabited sites by man. In 1921, close to Beijing were found the bones of a Sinanthrope, better known as "Peking Man", dead more than 500,000 years before our era, in the Neolithic period. It is the earliest sign of human being in this region. As a city, Beijing boasts a history of over 3,000 years, and as a capital city, a history of more than 1,000 years.

Situated in the northen part of China, the first urban districts of Beijing would remain confined to a role as a frontier town before gaining the continuing status of regional capital and then imperial capital. From the 7th century BC on, by different successive kingdoms, constructions of small protective walls had been undertaken, which gradually formed the Great Wall of China. It was not until Kublai Khan named it as the capital of the Yuan Dynasty did Beijing finally become the political centre of the whole country, playing a leading role in the Chinese history.

Early times from the Zhou Dynasty to the Jin Dynasty

Beijing was for a long time a small regional capital under

the Zhou and Jin dynasties. The construction of Beijing City dated back to the year of 1045 BC in Western Zhou Dynasty. It was first recorded as the city of "Ji" or "Jicheng". In 221BC, in the Qin Empire, the first unified feudal empire of China, it was an ordinary prefectural town, but had great strategic importance. In the 10th century, the Khitan, a Mongolian tribe in northern China, established the Liao Dynasty and occupied "Youzhou" (the name of Beijing at that time) in 936,. Then it was named Nanjing (Southern Capital) and then renamed "Yanjing" as a secondary capital of the Liao Dynasty. In 1115, the Nüzhen tribe in the northeastern China set up the Jin Dynasty with the capital in Huining (today's Heilongjiang Province). They occupied Yanjing in 1122 and moved their capital there in 1153, and then renamed it Zhongdu (Central Capital).

Yuan Dynasty

The troops of Genghis Khan, from 1213, launched the first raids on the Great Wall. In 1215, Genghis Khan finally penetrated Zhongdu and razed the city completely. Later, his grandson Kublai Khan, decided to make it the capital of the Yuan Dynasty, which was the beginning of the true rise of Beijing. In 1267, the rebuilt city got the name Khanbalik, "City of the Emperor", or Dadu in Chinese (Great Capital) and became

known in the West as "Cambaluc" thanks to the stories of Marco Polo.

Ming and Qing dynasties

In the beginning years of the Ming Dynasty, the capital of China was Naijing. Years later, Zhu Di, the third Ming Emperor, moved the capital to Beijing which then took its current name. It was also Zhu Di who ordered to rebuilt and enlarge Beijing City and constructed the Forbidden City. The other architectural achievements made during the Ming Dynasty were the Temple of Heaven, the Ming Tombs, the Great Bell Temple and so on. After the Qing Dynasty took power in 1644, Beijing remained the capital of China. The Qing emperors continued to improve the Forbidden City. The greatest achievement was vast complexes of the imperial gardens and palaces, such as the Summer Palace, the Garden of Perfection and Brightness, the Garden of Everlasting Spring and so on.

New China

After Chairman Mao Zedong solemnly proclaimed to the world the founding of the People's Republic of China, a new chapter of the city's history has opened up. Still maintaining its status as the capital of the whole country, Beijing has been developing very rapidly, especially after China's reform and opening-up policy was carried out. It has evolved into the political, cultural and economic centre of the country.

The city, with an immensive area of 16,808 square kilometres which is divided into 16 districts and two counties, and a dense population of permanent residents, in addition to 5,107 million floating population, is well on its way of fast development by blending fresh modern achievements with lingering traditional flavours together. Reflected in the glass walls of skyscrapers and office blocks are gilt roofs and scarlet walls of imperial palaces and gardens; besides expressways and trestles of bustling traffic are zigzagging narrow *hutong* where daily life of Beijinners hums with activity; high pitched Peking operas are played while at the same time hip-hop and rocks can be heard too. The charm of this mixture attracts every year millions of foreigners and still more Chinese to the city. Since Beijing's successful bid for the 2008 Olympic Games in 2001, the city has become more and more the focus of the world's attention and it has made even greater development. More than ever before, Beijing is open to the world with its historic heritage, modern developments and promising future.

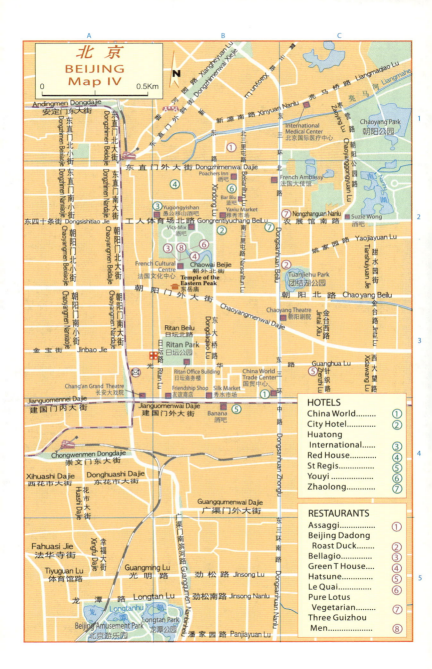

BEIJING
Map IV

0   0.5Km

HOTELS
China World........ ①
City Hotel............ ②
Huatong
 International...... ③
Red House............ ④
St Regis............... ⑤
Youyi .... ⑥
Zhaolong............ ⑦

RESTAURANTS
Assaggi............... ①
Beijing Dadong
 Roast Duck........ ②
Bellagio............... ③
Green T House.... ④
Hatsune.............. ⑤
Le Quai............... ⑥
Pure Lotus
 Vegetarian........ ⑦
Three Guizhou
 Men.................. ⑧

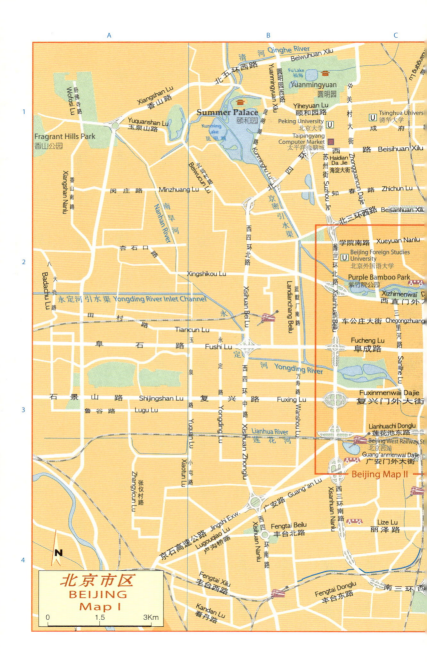

BEIJING Map I

北京市区
BEIJING
Map I

0   1.5   3Km

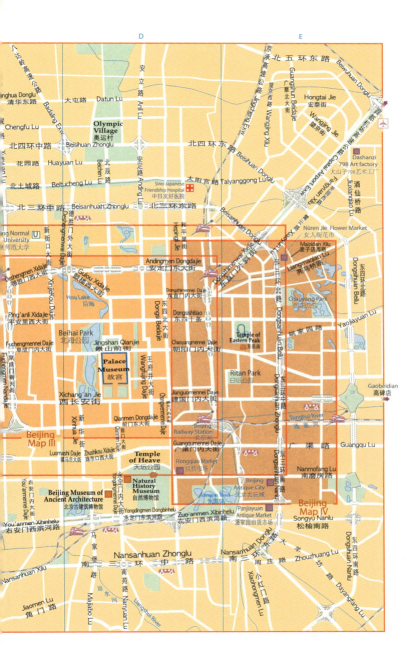

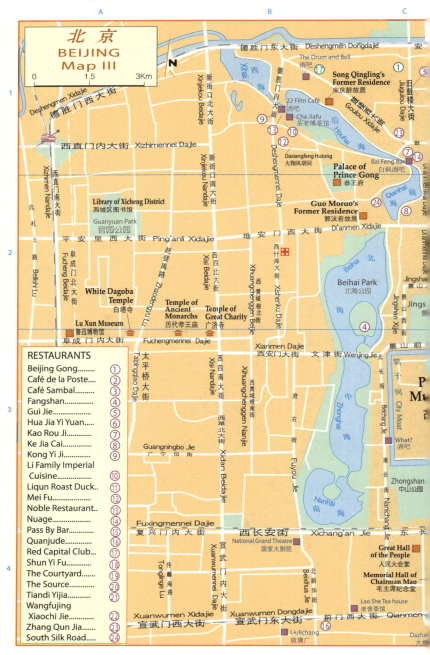

北京
BEIJING
Map III

0   1.5   3Km

N

Deshengmen Xidajie 德胜门西大街

Xizhimennei Dajie 西直门内大街

新街口北大街 Xinjiekou Beidajie

新街口南大街 Xinjiekou Nandajie

Deshengmen Dongdajie 德胜门东大街

The Drum and Bell
酒吧 ⑰

Song Qingling's
Former Residence
宋庆龄故居

旧鼓楼大街 Jiugulou Dajie ①

鼓楼东大街 Gulou Dongdajie

后门桥 Goulou Xidajie

22 Film Café
酒吧
Cha Jiafu
茶家傅茶馆 ⑩

Houhai 后海

Bai Feng Bar
白枫酒吧 ⑦ ⑭

Daxiangfeng Hutong
大翔风胡同

**Palace of
Prince Gong**
恭王府

⑨ ⑬ ⑫

Deshengmennei Dajie 德胜门内大街

Xihai 西海

Qianhai 前海 ⑧

**Guo Moruo's
Former Residence**
郭沫若故居 ㉔

Library of Xicheng District
西城区图书馆

Guanyuan Park
官园公园

Di'anmen Xidajie 地安门西大街

Ping'anli Xidajie 平安里西大街

赵登禹路 Zhaodengyu Lu

西四北大街 Xisi Beidajie

西什库大街 Xishiku Dajie

地安门西大街

西黄城根北大街 Xihuangchenggen Beijie

Bell Shi Lu 北礼士路

Fucheng Beidajie 阜成门北大街

Beihai Park
北海公园

Jingsha
景山

Jingshan Xijie 景山西街

Jings

**White Dagoba
Temple**
白塔寺

**Temple of
Ancient
Monarchs**
历代帝王庙

**Temple of
Great Charity**
广济寺

Xianmen Dajie 西安门大街

Wenjing Jie 文津街

Lu Xun Museum
鲁迅博物馆

Fuchengmennei Dajie 阜成门内大街

Fuchengmennei Dajie 阜成门内大街

RESTAURANTS

Beijing Gong.........	①
Café de la Poste....	②
Café Sambal..........	③
Fangshan..............	④
Gui Jie.................	⑤
Hua Jia Yi Yuan.....	⑥
Kao Rou Ji............	⑦
Ke Jia Cai.............	⑧
Kong Yi Ji.............	⑨
Li Family Imperial Cuisine..............	⑩
Liqun Roast Duck..	⑪
Mei Fu.................	⑫
Noble Restaurant..	⑬
Nuage..................	⑭
Pass By Bar...........	⑮
Quanjude..............	⑯
Red Capital Club...	⑰
Shun Yi Fu............	⑱
The Courtyard.......	⑲
The Source...........	⑳
Tiandi Yijia...........	㉑
Wangfujing Xiaochi Jie.............	㉒
Zhang Qun Jia.......	㉓
South Silk Road.....	㉔

太平桥大街 Taipingqiao Dajie

西四南大街 Xisi Nandajie

西黄城根南大街 Xihuangchenggen Nanjie

Guangningbo Jie 广宁伯街

西单北大街 Xidan Beidajie

府右街 Fuyou Jie

Zhonghai 中海

Beichang Jie 北长街

City Moat 筒子河

What?
酒吧

Zhongshan
中山公园

Nanchang Jie 南长街

P
Mu

Fuxingmennei Dajie 复兴门内大街

Nanhai 南海

西长安街 Xichang'an Jie

Xichang'an Jie 东长

**Great Hall
of the People**
人民大会堂

National Grand Theatre
国家大剧院

**Memorial Hall of
Chairman Mao**
毛主席纪念馆

Tonglinge Lu 佟麟阁路

佟麟阁路 Tonglinge Lu

宣武门内大街 Xuanwumennei Dajie

北新华街 Beixinhua Jie

Lao She Tea house
老舍茶馆 ㉒

Qianmen 前门

Xuanwumen Xidajie 宣武门西大街

宣武门西大街 Xuanwumen Xidajie

Xuanwumen Dongdajie 宣武门东大街

宣武门东大街

前门西大街 Qianmen

Dazha

Liulichang
琉璃厂 ⑯

A   B   C

1   2   3   4

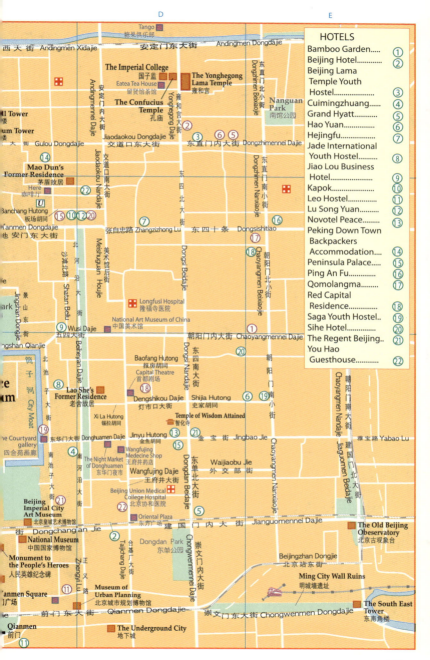

HOTELS

Bamboo Garden..... ①
Beijing Hotel............. ②
Beijing Lama Temple Youth Hostel................... ③
Cuimingzhuang........ ④
Grand Hyatt........... ⑤
Hao Yuan................ ⑥
Hejingfu................. ⑦
Jade International Youth Hostel........... ⑧
Jiao Lou Business Hotel................... ⑨
Kapok.................... ⑩
Leo Hostel............. ⑪
Lu Song Yuan........ ⑫
Novotel Peace......... ⑬
Peking Down Town Backpackers Accommodation.... ⑭
Peninsula Palace..... ⑮
Ping An Fu............. ⑯
Qomolangma......... ⑰
Red Capital Residence............... ⑱
Saga Youth Hostel.. ⑲
Sihe Hotel.............. ⑳
The Regent Beijing.. ㉑
You Hao Guesthouse........... ㉒

113

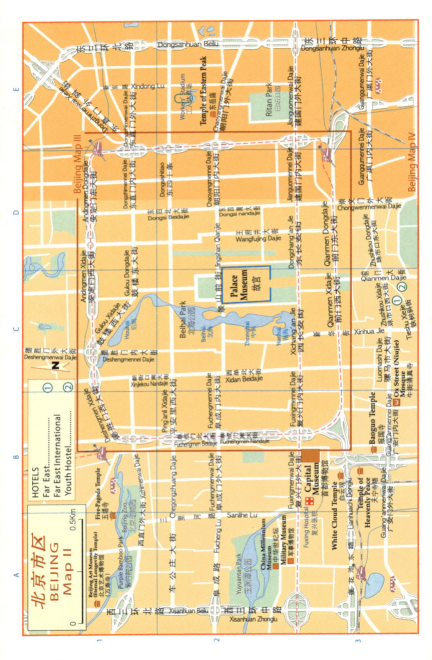

北京市区
BEIJING
Map II

0   0.5km

HOTELS
Far East............................①
Far East International
Youth Hostel....................②

N

Beijing Art Museum
(Eternal Longevity Temple)
北京艺术博物馆
(万寿寺)

Five-Pagoda Temple 五塔寺
Purple Bamboo Park 紫竹院公园
Beijing Zoo 北京动物园

**China Millennium
Museum**
中华世纪坛
Military Museum 军事博物馆

White Cloud Temple 白云观
Fuxing Hospital 复兴医院

**Capital
Museum**
首都博物馆

**Temple of
Heavenly Peace**
天宁寺

Baoguo Temple 报国寺

**Ox Street (Niujie)
Mosque** 牛街清真寺

Beijing Map III

Beijing Map IV

Dongsanhuan Beilu

Dongsanhuan Zhonglu

Xindong Lu

Workers' Stadium
工人体育场

Temple of Eastern Peak
东岳庙

Ritan Park 日坛公园

Chaoyangmenwai Dajie
朝阳门外大街

Jianguomenwai Dajie
建国门外大街

Guangqumenwai Dajie
广渠门外大街

Andingmen Dongdajie
安定门东大街

Dongzhimennei Dajie
东直门内大街

Dongsishitao
东四十条

Chaoyangmennei Dajie
朝阳门内大街

Jianguomennei Dajie
建国门内大街

Chongwenmenwai Dajie
崇文门外大街

Guangqumennei Dajie
广渠门内大街

Dongsi Beidajie
东四北大街

Dongsi nandajie
东四南大街

Wangfujing Dajie
王府井大街

Dongchang'an Jie
东长安街

Qianmen Dongdajie
前门东大街

Zhushikou Dongdajie
珠市口东大街

Zhushikou Xidajie
珠市口西大街

Tieshu Xiejie
铁树斜街

**Palace
Museum** 故宫

Jingshan Qianjie
景山前街

Xichang'an Jie
西长安街

Qianmen Xidajie
前门西大街

Xinhua Jie 新华街

Luomashi Dajie
骡马市大街

Andingmen Xidajie
安定门西大街

Gulou Dongdajie
鼓楼东大街

Beihai Park 北海公园

Zhonghai 中海

Nanhai 南海

Gulou Xidajie
鼓楼西大街

Houhai 后海

Deshengmenwai Dajie
德胜门外大街

Deshengmennei Dajie
德胜门内大街

Xinjiekou Nandajie
新街口南大街

Xidan Beidajie
西单北大街

Xinwen Dajie

Ping'an Xidajie
平安里西大街

Fuchengmennei Dajie
阜成门内大街

Fuxingmennei Dajie
复兴门内大街

Xizhimennwai Dajie
西直门外大街

Chegongzhuang Dajie
车公庄大街

Fuchengmenwai Dajie
阜成门外大街

Fuchengmen Beidajie
阜成门北大街

Fuchengmen Nandajie
阜成门南大街

Fuxingmennei Dajie
复兴门内大街

Fuxingmenwai Dajie
复兴门外大街

Guang'anmennei Dajie
广安门内大街

Guang'anmenwai Dajie
广安门外大街

Sanlihe Lu 三里河

Fucheng Lu 阜成路

Lianhuachi Donglu
莲花池东路

Yuyuantan Park 玉渊潭公园

Xisanhuan Beilu 西三环北路

Xisanhuan Zhonglu 西三环中路

114

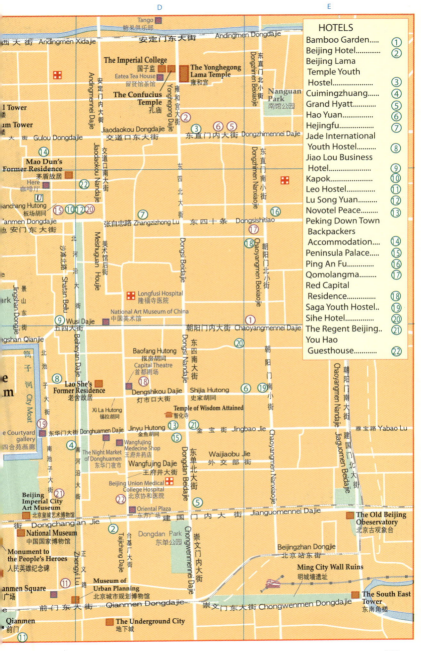

D   E

HOTELS

Bamboo Garden..... ①
Beijing Hotel............. ②
Beijing Lama
Temple Youth
Hostel.................... ③
Cuimingzhuang...... ④
Grand Hyatt............ ⑤
Hao Yuan................ ⑥
Hejingfu.................. ⑦
Jade International
Youth Hostel.......... ⑧
Jiao Lou Business
Hotel...................... ⑨
Kapok..................... ⑩
Leo Hostel.............. ⑪
Lu Song Yuan.......... ⑫
Novotel Peace......... ⑬
Peking Down Town
Backpackers
Accommodation.... ⑭
Peninsula Palace..... ⑮
Ping An Fu............. ⑯
Qomolangma......... ⑰
Red Capital
Residence............... ⑱
Saga Youth Hostel.. ⑲
Sihe Hotel.............. ⑳
The Regent Beijing.. ㉑
You Hao
Guesthouse............ ㉒

西 天 街 Andingmen Xidajie
安定门东大街 Andingmen Dongdajie
Tango 棕榈泉俱乐部

The Imperial College
国子监
Eatea Tea House
留贤馆茶馆
The Confucius Temple
孔庙
The Yonghegong Lama Temple
雍和宫

东直门北小街 Dongzhimen Beixiaojie

Nanguan Park
南馆公园

Andingmennei Dajie 安定门内大街

Yonghegong Dajie 雍和宫大街

Jiaodaokou Dongdajie
交道口东大街

东直门内大街 Dongzhimennei Dajie

l Tower
m Tower
街 Gulou Dongdajie

Jiaodaokou Nandajie 交道口南大街

东直门南小街 Dongzhimen Nanxiaojie

Mao Dun's Former Residence
茅盾故居
Here
咖啡厅

anchang Hutong
板场胡同
U

anmen Dongdajie
也 安门东大街

Shatan Beilu 沙滩北街 河 沿 大 街

Meishuguan Houjie 美术馆后街

Dongsi Beidajie 东四北大街

张自忠路 Zhangzizhong Lu   东四十条 Dongsishitiao

Dongsishitiao

朝阳门北小街 Chaoyangmen Beixiaojie

Longfusi Hospital
隆福寺医院
National Art Museum of China
中国美术馆

gshan Dongjie
park
gshan Qianjie

Beiheyan Dajie 北河沿大街

朝阳门内大街 Chaoyangmennei Dajie

Wusi Dajie 五四大街

Baofang Hutong
报房胡同
Capital Theatre
首都剧场

Dongsi Nandajie 东四南大街

朝 阳 门 南 小 街 Chaoyangmen Nanxiaojie

City Moat 筒 子 河 城 池

Lao She's Former Residence
老舍故居

Dengshikou Dajie
灯市口大街

Shijia Hutong
史家胡同

e Courtyard gallery
四合院画廊

东华门大街 Donghuamen Dajie

Xi La Hutong
锡拉胡同

Temple of Wisdom Attained
智化寺

Jinyu Hutong
金鱼胡同

金 宝 街 Jingbao Jie

Chaoyangmen Nanxiaojie

雅宝路 Yabao Lu

Wangfujing Medicine Shop
王府井药店

The Night Market of Donghuamen
东华门夜市

Wangfujing Dajie
王府井大街

Waijiaobu Jie
外 交 部 街

Jianguomen Beidajie 建国门北大街

Chaoyangmen Nandajie 朝阳门南大街

Beijing Union Medical College Hospital
北京协和医院

Beijing Imperial City Art Museum
北京皇城艺术博物馆

Oriental Plaza
东方广场 建 国 门 内 大 街 Jianguomennei Dajie

The Old Beijing Obeservatory
北京古观象台

Dongdan Beidajie 东单北大街

Dongchang'an Jie 东长安街

National Museum
中国国家博物馆

Monument to the People's Heroes
人民英雄纪念碑

anmen Square
广场

Zhengyi Lu 正 义 路

Taijichang Dajie 台基厂大街

Dongdan Park
东单公园

Chongwenmennei Dajie 崇文门内大街

Beijingzhan Dongjie
北京站东街

Museum of Urban Planning
北京城市规划博物馆

Ming City Wall Ruins
明城墙遗址

The South East Tower
东南角楼

Qianmen
前门

The Underground City
地下城

前 门 东 大 街 Qianmen Dongdajie

崇 文 门 东 大 街 Chongwenmen Dongdajie

113

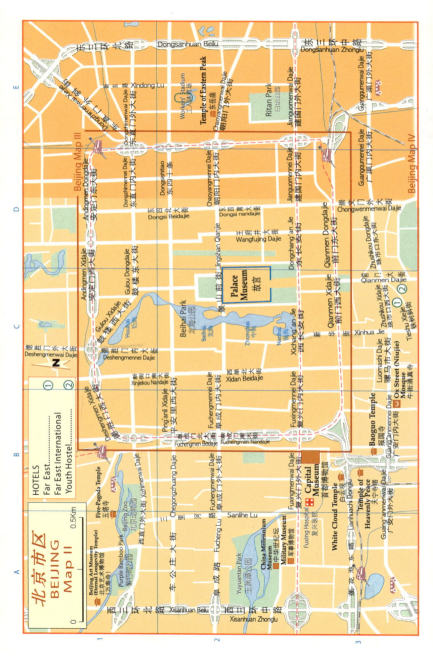

北京市区
BEIJING
Map II

HOTELS
Far East.......................①
Far East International
Youth Hostel............②

0   0.5Km

Beijing Map III

Beijing Map IV

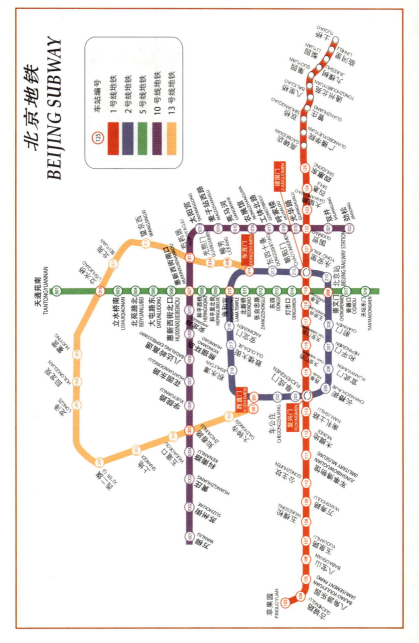

北京地铁
BEIJING SUBWAY

Walking Tours

1 The Forbidden City and Wangfujing   118

2 Around Deshengmen   140

3 Sanlitun and Chaoyang District   150

4 Around Dongzhimen   157

5 South of Qianmen   163

6 West Beijing   175

7 Around Beijing   189

8 The Great Wall and the Imperial Tombs 195

WALKING TOURS

Walking Tour 1:
The Forbidden City and Wangfujing

Map III, p112.

This walking tour allows you to discover the most important monument in Beijing, even in the whole of China: the Forbidden City. This constitutes not only the geographical centre of Beijing, but also, in Chinese history, the centre of the country. You cannot imagine a visit to the capital without allowing yourself at least half a day to visit the Forbidden City, preferably early in the morning.

If you have a whole day to spare, you could take advantage of the time and complete this walk by visiting monuments and places situated at the centre of the square, such as the Memorial Hall of Chairmen Mao and the Monument to the People's Heroes, or those bordering it: from one side to the other, to the west the Great Hall of the People, and to the east, the National Museum of China.

The following is the recommended itinerary: start the visit by discovering Tian'anmen Square, the largest public space in the world, and then enter the Forbidden City from the south, through Tian'anmen Gate. After this visit, leave the Forbidden City to the north and make your way to Coal Hill, from the top of which you will have a superb view over the roofs of the Forbidden City. Then after a well-deserved lunch,

return towards Tian'anmen Square to visit its monuments. At the end of the day, you will be present at the changing of the guard or the flag lowering ceremony. In the evening's completely changing atmosphere, you will have the pleasure of discovering Wangfujing, located parallel to the Forbidden City on the east side. This great popular commercial thoroughfare is the equivalent of the Champs-Elysées in France, Oxford Street in UK or Fifth Avenue in US.

Or, better still, Qianmen Dajie, located to the south of the Qianmen Gate. Six centuries old, but currently under reconstruction, this street is to be open to the public before the Olympic Games.

How then to explore Tian'anmen Square and the Forbidden City? You can't arrive from any side you like. To take in the scale of its whole architecture and exceptional spirituality, you have to enter from the south and keep moving north-wards. Before setting off, don't forget to put in your bag a cap and sunglasses in summer or warm clothes in winter, a large bottle of water and some dried fruit, and warm your feet appropriately: this walk represents a distance of 8 to 12 kilometres, indeed longer if you retrace your steps along the way.

To get to the Qianmen Gate, the easiest way is to get into a taxi. If the prospect of a long walk puts you off or if you have too little time, go by underground: Tian'anmen East Station and Tian'anmen West Station both are located in front of the south entry to the Forbidden City.

The visit starts therefore at the foot of the Qianmen Gate, on the south side of Tian'anmen Square.

Qianmen Gate

前门
Map III, C4
Tel (010) 65229382
8:30am—4pm/10 yuan

Located at the south end of Tian'anmen Square, the enormous Qianmen Gate (the Front Gate), was erected at the start of the 15th century by Emperor Chengzu. Originally a wall stood to both sides of this gate, but today it stands isolated on a grassy roundabout. It gives a good view on Tian'anmen Square.

Tian'anmen Square

天安门广场
Map III, C4

Tian'anmen Square takes its name from the gate of the same name situated at the north end of the square, and gives access to the Forbidden City.

Let's take a small etymological detour to better understand the metaphysical dimension of this site. The simplest character in the Chinese language is "*yī*", which is written with a single straight horizontal line: "一", and which means "one". It's the perfect character, which embodies, if you will, the original unit. Let's now break this original unit into two pieces of equal length. With these two strokes joined at the top, you can form another fundamental character, "*rén*", which is written as "人" and means "man". In fact, this character seems to represent both legs of a walking man. Let's go further. To conjure up in the mind something big, the Chinese add a horizontal stroke to the character "*rén*", a kind of pair of arms to show size: it's the character "*dà*", written as "大". Let's now add another stroke to this character, a stroke above it all, a stroke which brings to mind something even greater than man and almost inaccessible to him, but is all the

same connected to him: it's the character "*tiān*", which means "heaven", but can also have the meaning of "cosmic nature", and is written as "天".

For the Chinese the names of places and things are more important than the things and places themselves. So, you can see, the character "*tiān*" already gives a sense of space and spirituality. The same goes for the second character of the name "Tian'anmen", the character "*ān*", "安". This character represents a woman (*nǔ*, 女) housed under a roof; it means "peace". The third, "*mén*", "門", is strictly speaking a pictogram: it represents the design of a traditional Chinese door (the lateral uprights are closed off by two flaps halfway up) and means "door".

Crossing Tian'anmen square and progressing from Qianmen Gate towards Tian'anmen gate, you are therefore at the same time passing through real gates, which are the masterpieces of military architecture, but also symbolic gates which take you from the secular world to the world of harmony. Once over this threshold, thanks to the intercession of the Emperor, the perfect balance of the forces of nature, the "yīn" (阴) and the "yáng" (阳) is established. But, before it was an architectural masterpiece, the Forbidden City (along with Beijing's other monuments which complement and complete the picture) constituted first the centre of earthly and celestial power, a metaphysical construction on which the past, present and future of the people of the Empire depend for hundreds of years.

Memorial Hall of Chairman Mao

毛主席纪念堂
Map III, C4
Tel (010) 65132277
Tues.—Sun.: 8:30am—11:30am;
Tues., Thurs.: 2pm—4pm
Access to the Memorial hall is free, but you must leave your belongings at the left luggage counter (3 yuan for a bag. 5 yuan each for valuables: camera, handbag...).

It's not difficult to see this imposing concrete cube placed at the centre of the square, as a counterpoint to the Forbidden City. It's a quasi-ritual place to visit for the Chinese coming from the distant confines of the country. It is mandatory to maintain proper behaviour around the memorial hall, all the more so when inside. The queue to enter the memorial hall is very long, but it moves quickly. It is forbidden to stop in front of the Monument to the People's Heroes and guards are used to moving the queue on quickly. Photographs are not permitted and you must leave all your belongings without exception at the left luggage desk which you will find on the other side of the square, the east side. Don't be tempted to keep a bag with you: the guards constantly watch the queue and nothing escapes them. Coming out of the Memorial Hall, a shop is available for those who wish to acquire all sorts of items evoking the memory of Chairman Mao.

Monument to the People's Heroes

人民英雄纪念碑
MapIII, C4

Located to the north of the Memorial Hall of Chairman Mao, this 38-metre tall obelisk was erected in 1958. Its bas-reliefs are illustrated in a realist style typical of the great age of the Revolution since the Opium Wars. They correspond to the sculptures which frame the north entrance to the Memorial Hall of Chairman Mao. And like the Memorial Hall, it is guarded day and night by soldiers. You can only look at it by walking round, without going up to it. Be certain that guarding this monument is seen as a huge responsibility and a great honour: at all times be respectful to the young sentries.

National Museum of China

中国国家博物馆
Map III, C4
Tel (010) 65129335
www.nmch.gov.cn
8:30am—4:30pm, ticket office closes at 3:30pm/30 yuan

On the east side of Tian'anmen Square, the National Museum of China brings together the collections of two former Museums of History and of the Revolution. Undergoing renovation work at the time of our research, masked behind huge boards, this museum will re-open its doors in 2010. On the west side of the museum, a gigantic clock counts down the days to the opening of the Olympic Games.

The Great Hall of the People

人民大会堂

Map III, C4

Tel (010) 63096156
Jan., Mar., Dec.: 9am—2pm; Apr., Jun.: 8:15am—3pm; Jul., Aug.: 7:30am—4pm; Sep., Nov.:8:30am—3pm/30 yuan

Opposite the National Museum, on the other side of Tian'anmen Square, stands the immense People's Assembly, known simply as the Hall of the People. This enormous building inaugurated in 1959 never ceases to arouse the admiration of the people from the provinces. You can visit outside parliamentary sessions to discover, by the light of huge chandeliers, vast rooms with marble walls, where, for once, the megaphones used by the Chinese guides are turned down to zero volume. Each room bears the name of a Chinese province; with decorations to reflect its specific character. Most of the time you can only go as far as a small perimeter around the entrance, beyond which it is forbidden to go any further. During your visit you will go through the giant auditorium, capable of accommodating more than 10,000 members of the assembly, and the banqueting halls where Richard Nixon was invited to dine on the occasion of the first visit of a US President to the People's Republic of China in 1972.

Tian'anmen Rostrum

天安门城楼
Map III, C4
Tel (010) 63095745
8:30am—5pm, ticket office closes at 4:30pm/15 yuan

Before buying your ticket, you must leave all your personal belongings at the left luggage counter, located on the left just after the entrance. You can of course keep your camera. Be aware that you can leave your things for a maximum 1 hour: after that you will have to pay a (modest) supplement.

Marking the boundary between Tian'anmen Square and the Forbidden City, Tian'anmen Rostrum is adorned with a portrait of Mao Zedong and red flags draped over. It is the central point of the regime's official ceremonies, processions and other anniversaries, when dignitaries amass on the steps below opposite the square. It was from the top of the balcony on this gate that, on 1st October 1949, Mao Zedong proclaimed the founding of the People's Republic of China after his victory over the troops of Chiang Kai-shek (Jiang Jieshi). The interior houses several antiques and pieces of furnitures. Two television screens permanently show the great military parades which have lit up the square since 1949. Nevertheless, from the top of the rostrum you get a perfect view of the whole of the square. Best visited early in the morning before rush hour. Besides, the soft morning light gives the buildings an increased softness and elegance which is not superfluous.

Going from Tian'anmen Rostrum towards the Forbidden City, you have the possibility to visit Duanmen (9am—4:20pm/10 yuan), then Meridian Gate, finally the Gate of Supreme Harmony (access subject to any temporary exhibitions). Nevertheless, none can offer as interesting a view as you get from the top of Tian'anmen Rostrum.

Zhongshan Park

中山公园
Map III, C3—4
Tel (010) 66055431
May.—Oct.: 6am—10pm;
Nov.—Feb.: 6:30am—8:30pm;
Mar.—May.: 6am—9pm/3 yuan

This pleasant little park, situated to the west of the south gate of the Forbidden City houses the Sun Yat-sen Memorial Hall (9am—4pm/extra charge: 2 yuan) where several photographs and personal effects of the first President of the Republic of China have been preserved. Note as well in this park a vast round altar built by the Ming Emperor Chengzu at the same time as the Forbidden City. Emperors would come here twice a year to offer sacrifices to the God of Harvests.

Beijing Planning Exhibition Hall

北京市规划展览馆
Map III, CD—4
Tel (010) 67024559
9am—4pm/Closed Monday/30 yuan

Erected in a modern building, this museum is located south of Tian'anmen Square. We'd recommend a visit at the end of your stay in Beijing, when you will have become quite familiar with the city, to have it presented to you in its entirety. Don't expect an exhibition of ancient cultural relics: this educational museum is an introduction to the general public of the urban changes of today's Beijing. On the first floor there are photographs of old Beijing and the *hutong*. A giant model (several hundred square metres!) of the city occupies almost the

Working People's Cultural Palace

劳动人民文化宫
Tel (010) 65122103
6:30am—8:30pm/2 yuan

This vast park, with a small river running through, stretches to the southeast of the Forbidden City, passes Tian'anmen Rostrum. You'll choose to enjoy a little calm after visits to the Forbidden City or Tian'anmen Square. The Working People's Cultural Palace is above all known for its rows of ancient cypresses, several centuries old. Some interesting temporary exhibitions are held here.

whole of the floor, showing how the city looks in 2008: many people come to check if their house will still be there! The museum also includes models of the business district, the Olympic Village and the airport's Terminal 3, as well as a show-flat in futuristic style with new towers. Finally a movie in 3D retraces the city's history. There are often explanations translated into English.

The Forbidden City

故宫

Map III. C3.

Tel (010) 65132255

Apr.1—Oct.14: 8:30am—5pm, ticket office closes at 4pm, 60 yuan; Nov.—Mar.: 8:30am—3:30pm, 40 yuan; Audio guide: 40 yuan; deposit required: a form of identity (passport, etc.) or hotel key

Give yourself 2 hours if you follow the audio guide and keep to the northsouth direction of the tour. Add a further 2 hours to visit the halls alongside. A visit to the Forbidden City usually runs from north to south. You can enter for free as far as the Meridian Gate (午门), where tickets are sold and audio guides rented.

The building of this immense city, which was to act as imperial residence as well as seat of power, began in 1406, in the reign of Emperor Chengzu of the Ming Dynasty, and was completed 14 years later. The foundations of the old imperial city were used for the work. The Forbidden City remained the imperial residence for the Ming and Qing dynasties until 1911, the date of the declaration of the Republic of China. It was turned into a museum in 1925. The total surface area of the city covers 70 hectares (or twice the ground surface area of the Vatican in Rome). It is said that the palace has 9999 rooms. However, only a tiny part, restored and maintained can be visited. The palace could house almost 10,000 people: eunuchs and concubines who constituted one third of the Forbidden City's population.

The palace is formed of two distinct parts: the interior courtyard to the north, and the outer courtyard to the south. The empress entered the city from the north where the imperial couple had reserved quarters. The southern entrance with its five marble bridges crossing the Golden Water (金水河), was intended for the emperor, government dignitaries and ambassadors. The pillars of the bridge are sculpted in the form of torches, symbolising fire.

The Gate of Supreme Harmony (太和门), without doubt the most richly decorated in the city is guarded by two impressive

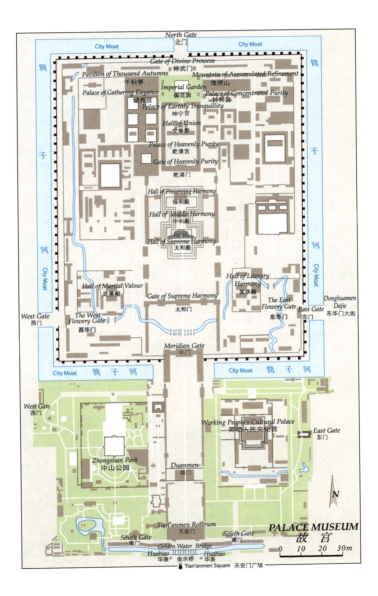

City Moat

North Gate
北门

City Moat

筒
子
河

筒
子
河

Gate of Divine Prowess
神武门

Pavilion of Thousand Autumns
千秋亭

Palace of Gathering Elegance
储秀宫

Imperial Garden
御花园

Mountain of Accumulated Refinement
堆绣山

Palace of Concentrated Purity
钟粹宫

Palace of Earthly Tranquillity
坤宁宫

Hall of Union
交泰殿

Palace of Heavenly Purity
乾清宫

Gate of Heavenly Purity
乾清门

Hall of Preserving Harmony
保和殿

Hall of Middle Harmony
中和殿

Hall of Supreme Harmony
太和殿

Hall of Martial Valour
武英殿

Gate of Supreme Harmony
太和门

Hall of Literary Harmony
文华殿

The East Flowery Gate
东华门

East Gate
东门

Donghuamen Dajie
东华门大街

West Gate
西门

The West Flowery Gate
西华门

City Moat 筒 子 河

Meridian Gate
午门

City Moat 筒 子 河

West Gate
西门

Zhongshan Park
中山公园

Duanmen
端门

Working People's Cultural Palace
劳动人民文化宫

East Gate
东门

Tian'anmen Rostrum
天安门

South Gate
南门

PALACE MUSEUM
故宫

South Gate
南门

Golden Water Bridge
金水桥

Huabiao
华表

Huabiao
华表

0 10 20 30m

N

Tian'anmen Square 天安门广场

131

gold lions. These lions, found in many temples and palaces, were the mark of the State's highest dignitaries. The lion on the right is male, holding a ball under its right paw, while the lion on the left is female and holds a lion cub under its left paw. The Gate of Supreme Harmony is not original. It was erected first in 1420, and then rebuilt completely under the Qing after being burnt in 1888. The rosewood ceilings are decorated entirely with golden dragons, the symbol of the emperor, and the door assembly was put together without any screws or nails. This door opens out onto the outer courtyard.

The outer courtyard, which occupies the southern part of the Forbidden City, was reserved for affairs of state. At its centre is the Hall of Supreme Harmony (太和殿), the most imposing building in the palace. It houses the emperor's throne (御座), finely carved, very richly decorated and covered in fine gold. You get there by a three level terrace one on top of the other, the steps of which are guarded by 1,100 dragons. Visitors are not allowed into the hall; you can look at the throne only from outside. The terrace is decorated in imperial symbols such as bronze cranes (symbolising long life) or a sundial. This palace, which on several occasions has been destroyed by fire, has been identically rebuilt and so looks the same as it did in 1420. The last rebuilding was in 1695. During that period of time, the biggest ceremonies, such as the emperor's birthday or Chinese New Year, were held in this palace and on this terrace in particular.

Right behind it is the Hall of Middle Harmony (中和殿), and the Hall of Preserving Harmony (保和殿). In the Hall of Middle Harmony, the emperor prepared matters which he would have to deal with that day. The Hall of Preserving Harmony was reserved for banquets and other grand ceremonies. Then, from 1789 this palace served as an examination room for the imperial exams.

In the following small courtyard, marvel at the marble ramp leading to the Gate of Heavenly Purity (乾清门). The ramp weighs more than 200 tons and was brought there in one single piece, thanks to a route specially constructed for the purpose. Trimmed with cornices, soaked and frozen in winter, it allowed the ramp to slide for dozens of kilometres without breaking. The door marks the boundary between the outer and inner courtyards. To the north the imperial couple led a private life away from prying eyes. Only members of the family, concubines, eunuchs and servants were admitted into this part of the city. A total of no less than 12 halls were needed, spread out to the east and west of the inner courtyard, to accommodate all these people.

Access to the three halls is from the rear by a private terrace reserved for the emperor and bearing the same symbols as that in the outer courtyard. The first is the Palace of Heavenly Purity (乾清宫). In the Ming period, some matters of the state were dealt with here. Under the Qing, the palace was entirely dedicated to the emperor's bedchamber. Immediately behind, the Hall of Union (交泰殿), was the quarter reserved for the empress. She had apartments there, as well as her throne,

always visible. Note the many phoenixes, symbol of the empress, which take the place of the dragons, symbol of the emperor.

The Palace of Earthly Tranquillity (坤宁宫), is striking in its different architectural and decorative style. It was destroyed by the Manchurians themselves when they took the Forbidden City and rebuilt at the start of the Qing Dynasty. This palace, where the imperial bed chamber of the imperial couple is found, was then turned into a place of worship to the west and wedding room to the east. The symbol of the couple and happiness still figures on the doors.

A visit to the Forbidden City ends with the Imperial Garden (御花园). Trees, flowers, rock falls, and cool air: all was put into operation to help the emperor feel at peace. At the centre of the garden is the Imperial Peace Hall (钦安殿). Note the two superb bronze unicorns which mark the entrance. You leave the Forbidden City by the north gate, the Gate of Divine Prowess (神武门).

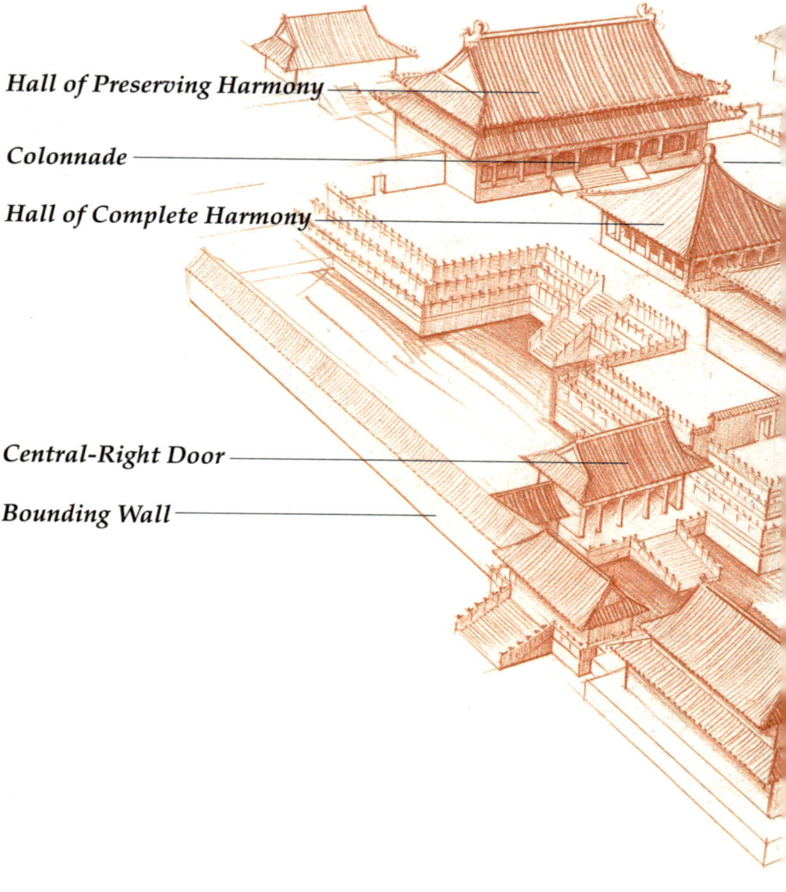

Hall of Preserving Harmony

Colonnade

Hall of Complete Harmony

Central-Right Door

Bounding Wall

Palace Museum-Beijing

Three Main Halls

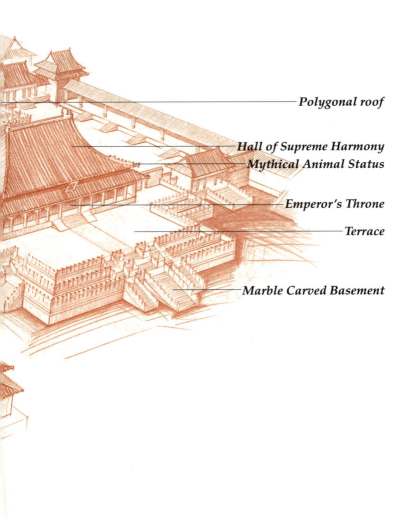

Polygonal roof

Hall of Supreme Harmony

Mythical Animal Status

Emperor's Throne

Terrace

Marble Carved Basement

Coal Hill Park

景山公园

Tel (010) 64044071
6:30am—8pm in winter, 6am—9pm
from spring to autumn, 6am—10pm in
summer/2 yuan

Situated directly to the north of the Forbidden City, on the other side of the road with regard to the Gate of Divine Prowess which marks the northern limit of the Forbidden City, Coal Hill Park is one of the most pleasant parks in Beijing. It doubles as an excellent viewpoint over the city centre, particularly the Forbidden City and its gilded roofs, with Tian'anmen Square in the background. The hill is man-made. It was erected during the Yuan Dynasty with earth taken from the moats of the first imperial city and the artificial lakes. It's here where the last Ming Emperor died. He hung himself from a tree in the park just as Li Zicheng's army were entering the Forbidden City in 1644, thus putting an end to his dynasty. From the top of the hill, you look down on the *hutong* and can make out the Bell and Drum towers, the pagoda of Beihai Park next door, as well as the White Dagoba Temple, further west. Sunday morning, at dawn, the park is very lively. Beijingers take part in various different activities there (physical exercises, dancing, singing, musical instruments, calligraphy, families taking walks…) and won't hesitate to chat with you. In Chinese of course!

138

Wangfujing Dajie and Qianmen Dajie

王府井大街和前门大街

Wangfujing Dajie, is the equivalent of the Champs-Elysées in Paris, but busier. In the past, this road was lined with shops and workshops working mainly for the imperial palace. It housed artists and craftsmen of renown. It was rebuilt between 1996 and 1999 and partly pedestrianised, and has become a place of massive and prestigious consumption. Provincial Chinese coming to visit the Forbidden City like to stroll along here in the evening. A crowd of hawkers, pedlars and market traders give it a permanent festival atmosphere. Here and there, you get offered several amazing specialities to taste: for example, grilled scorpions...

Qianmen Dajie is the other great historical shopping street in the area of the Forbidden City. It is situated south of Tian'anmen Square, very lively and picturesque. This is the only way before arriving at Qianmen Gate. It was for the most part rebuilt in 2006—2007. Reconstruction is in progress. Several old buildings have been restored, blending the preserved with the new. The street is due to open in summer 2008. If you go down Qianmen Dajie towards Tian'anmen Square on the south, don't miss branching off at Dashilan Road. This narrow road is very lively and has kept a large part of its architectural heritage and charm.

WALKING TOURS

Walking Tour 2:
Around Deshengmen

Here is a walking tour which allows you to discover one of the best preserved quarters in old Beijing. Ideally you would travel by bicycle, for distances between the sites are long on foot, and often bottlenecked. It's possible to bypass the big axes of traffic by using the alleyways which wind along the *hutong*, which increases the charm of this walk. It's also an opportunity to engage unexpectedly with the nice people of the quarter, who from the first signs of spring, live for the most part in the street amongst neighbours. The starting point for this walking tour is the Drum Tower, located at the northern edge of the Imperial City of the Yuan Dynasty.

Drum Tower

鼓楼
MapIII, C1
9am—4:30pm/20 yuan
Drum demonstration every half hour from 9am to 11:30am and from 1pm to 4:30pm

Beijing's Drum Tower was erected in 1420 in the Ming Dynasty. It measures 47 metres high and at that time marked the northern boundary of the city. The beating of the drums announced the closing of the city

gates. The building was entirely rebuilt under the Qing in 1745. Its massive three-floor construction of tiled roofs today offers a pretty viewpoint over the old parts of Beijing. You can see in particular the significance of the tree garden scattered throughout private courtyards, not visible from the street. Besides it is possible to go around the whole floor from the outside, unlike the Bell Tower where you have to be content with what you can see through the porches on the sides. A particularly steep 69 steps give you access to the level where 21 drums are placed (the tower had 25 originally). The main drum was deliberately pierced by the Eight-Power Allied Forces when they took Beijing in 1900 and has been preserved in the same state.

Bell Tower

钟楼

MapIII, C1

9am—5pm/15 yuan

It is situated to the north of the Drum Tower (the trip cannot be made on foot, or at least by pedicab, many of which can be found in this tourist quarter). It takes 75 steps to get to the top of this 33 metres high tower, erected in the 18th century. The interesting view is the one which overlooks the Drum Tower, better developed in terms of attractiveness. The size of the main bell is impressive (63 tons, 3.40 metres in diameter, 7 metres high), but bears neither decoration nor any writing. A twenty-minute visit will suffice.

Beihai Park

北海公园

Map III, B—C2

Tel (010)64033225

Apr.—Oct.: 6am—9pm; Nov.—Mar 6:30am—8pm/Apr.—Oct.:10 yuan, 20 yuan with guide, Nov.—March:5 yuan

Situated to the northwest of the Forbidden City, this park houses Beihai Lake (North Lake), developed during the Yuan Dynasty. The emperors used to come to look for a few moments of relaxation in these 70 hectares mostly covered by water. There are four entrances to the park. The South gate leads to a bridge allowing you to reach the Jade Islet where the Yong'an Temple (永安寺; same hours as the park; supplement: 10 yuan).

urn in the world. This dates from 1265 and weighs 3.5 tons. This magnificent piece is decorated with lavish sculptures of mythical creatures and is worth the detour. It was used to hold wine at the huge banquets organised by the Emperor Kublai Khan.

Other interesting buildings justify the visit to the park right up to its north edge (charming palace, landscaped gardens). Very often on Saturday and Sunday this park is a valued place for socialising for Beijingers.

Mei Lanfang's Former Residence

梅兰芳故居
Map III, B1
Tel (010) 66183598
www.meilanfang.com.cn
9am—4pm/Closed Monday/10 yuan
The former personal residence of

and its White Dagoba (白塔). This Tibetan style temple, erected in 1651 on the occasion of a visit by the Dalai Lama, dominates the whole Park with its height of 36 metres. The northeast shore of the Islet is lined with a covered gallery beautifully decorated and painted.

For an extra 1 yuan, you can enter the Round City (same hours as the Park). With a surface area of 4,533 square metres, it's simply the smallest city on the world, which as its another oddity contains the largest jade

Mei Lanfang is situated 20 metres to the west of the crossroads of Deshengmennei Dajie and Huguosi Dajie. Mei Lanfang (1894—1961) gave his life to Peking Opera, and he was known for his talent in female roles. In the first hall there are numerous photographs of the artist in Peking Opera, but also snaps taken during overseas tours. Two other halls show works from various artists in respect of Mei Lanfang and works from the artist himself. At the end of the courtyard is his house, which has preserved the furniture of the time. Even if you are not taken by the opera, swing by this tiny residence to get an exact idea of what the inside of a traditional house in the Beijing *hutong* is like: it's a rare example of one still preserved and open to the public.

Palace of Prince Gong

恭王府
Map III, B2
Tel (010)66168149
Winter: 8:30am—4:30pm; Summer: 8:30am—5pm/20 yuan, 60 yuan with guide

Prince Gong's residence, built in the last quarter of the 18th century covering an area of 3 hectares, merits a long detour for the magnificence of its gardens. Stone forests, underground passages, small lakes and fountains, all conceived according to the rules of *fengshui*. This wisely organised artificial landscape is aimed to enchant its visitors. Some rooms, where short dance and music shows are organised, are open only to groups. An elegant tearoom is housed in the Futing Hall.

Guo Moruo's Former Residence

郭沫若纪念馆
Map III, C2
Tel (010) 66125392
9am—4:30pm/Closed Monday/20 yuan

Guo Moruo (1892—1978), a famous writer and poet, became director of the Chinese Academy of Sciences in 1949 and held in the following two decades several prestigious posts. His residence, which is in fact an annex of Prince Gong's Palace, has been preserved in its original state. The furniture of the era

has been preserved, as has a large collection of photographs, many manuscripts and various books. The internal garden is a veritable haven of peace.

Song Qingling's Former Residence

宋庆龄故居
Map III, B1
Tel (010) 64035858
9am—4pm/Closed Monday and Wednesday/20 yuan

From 1949 on, the Chinese government set out to look for a house for Song Qingling, better known as the widow of Sun Yat-sen, and presented with the title of Honorary President of the People's Republic of China. Song Qingling (1893—1981) lived the final 18 years of her life in this pretty dwelling, set in a vast park of the north bank of Houhai Lake. It is in fact the former palace of Prince Zai Feng. It's here where

the last Qing Emperor, Puyi, was born (about whom the film *The Last Emperor* traces his life story). There isn't much left of the palace, replaced by a modern house specially built for Song Qingling who moved here in 1963, but the park, which is pleasantly landscaped, maintains a certain charm. Inside, you can visit large reception rooms, banquet halls as well as the rooms where Song Qingling took care of the children of her Foundation. The universe of the wife of Sun Yat-sen is held in high value: the rooms are visible from the corridors, not through small windows as with other residences, and all information is translated into English. An outdated atmosphere emanates from this place, which only adds to its charm.

Lao She's Former Residence

老舍纪念馆
Map III, D3
Tel (010) 65142612
9am—5pm/10 yuan

To get there, leave from the east gate of the Forbidden City and turn left on Beiheyan Dajie as far as Dengshixikou and turn right; then take the second *hutong* on the left.

Lao She, seen as the greatest writer in Beijing—if not in China—from the last century, lived in this small traditional house in the heart of the capital's old *hutong*, east of the Forbidden City.

The first room brings together numerous photographs and books by Lao She published in various languages and editions, as well as drawings and personal items. The second room lets you see the writer's library. At the end of the courtyard lies his office. A block calendar, kept open at 24th August 1966, recalls the tragic suicide of the writer who threw himself into a lake. Next a small living room and Lao She's bedroom, very sober and furnished with the basic necessities. The journey comes to an end in a small souvenir shop where you can find books by Lao She and films made based on his works. This site is well preserved, full of charm and intimacy.

Lao She

Born in 1899 in Beijing, Lao She, whose real name was Shu Qingchun, followed a classic teaching career before knowing success with his novel: *The Rickshaw Boy* (《骆驼祥子》). His most famous work *Four Generations in one household* (《四世同堂》) describes the privations of Beijing residents under Japanese occupation. After the founding of New China, Lao She became attached to writing numerous plays, of which the most well-known, Teahouse, achieved great success in 1956. His autobiographical novel *Under the Pure Red Flag* (《正红旗下》), begun in 1961, remained unfinished.

Mao Dun's Former Residence

茅盾故居
Map III, C2
Tel (010) 64044089
9am—4pm/Closed Monday,
Wednesday and Friday/5 yuan.

From the Drum Tower walk for 400 metres towards the east until you reach Nanluogu Xiang then take right down the first *hutong* (indicated by a red sign), branch off into the fourth *hutong* on the left.

This traditional house with red and green walls and with a grey slate roof was the residence of Mao Dun (1896—1981), real name Shen Yanbing, writer of the realist movement. Like Lao She and Lu Xun, Mao Dun favoured short stories and novels having as background Chinese society of the 1920s. He had great success at the beginning of the 1930s with *Midnight* (《子夜》) and *Spring Silkworm* (《春蚕》). After a short desert crossing during the "cultural revolution", he briefly took up his pen again in the 1970s. The main rooms, library and lounge, are laid out around a central courtyard, but visible only from the outside. Only two rooms are open to the public, one containing several books and personal photographs of Mao Dun, the other showing the writer at official ceremonies.

Walking Tour 3:
Sanlitun and Chaoyang District

Chaoyang is the largest district in Beijing. It is a quarter going through a complete change. This area was once reserved for Embassies, but in the past 10 years or so, it has become Beijing's business and chic residential quarter. It's also the expats quarter, all nations mixed up, and the quarter for contemporary art galleries. Cafés, bars, restaurants, shops: all more expensive than elsewhere in Beijing. Useless to look for any trace of traditional local life in this quarter, it's for work and "chic" nights out. Nevertheless, some tourist sites do merit the detour, such as the Temple of the Eastern Peak or the old Ming City Wall Ruins.

How to get there

Map II, p. 148.

Sanlitun can be found to the west of Chaoyang District. It is a quarter at odds, where modern constructions stand side by side with old buildings, the demolition of which has begun. It is quite a pity, as these buildings from the 1950's and 1960's, made from red or yellow-brown brick, lack neither charm nor gentleness.

The nearest access points by underground are Dongzhimen and Dongsishitiao stations, from where you'll still need a walk of 10 minutes or so towards the east. Bus 115 links Di'anmen Dongdajie, to the north of Coal Hill Park (景山公园), and Sanlitun via the Workers'Stadium. From the centre, reckon on about 20 yuan by taxi.

WALKING TOURS

Ming City Wall Ruins Park

明城墙遗址公园
Map III, E4
Tel (010) 65270574

This site is particularly interesting for the atmosphere it generates. The remains of the old wall from the Ming Dynasty stretch along a straight line of 1.5 kilometres along Chongwenmen Dongdajie. This wall was erected in 1419 and formed part of a square enclosure 40 Kilometres long encircling Beijing. Even if it is only a small part of the old fortification, it gives you an idea of the colossal dimensions of the monument.

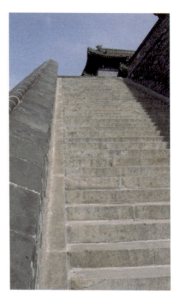

Southeast Tower

东南角楼

Map III, E4

9am—4:30pm/10 yuan

At one end of the wall stands a massive tower, which originally marked the southeast corner of the Ming wall. You can get there through an archway hollowed out of the wall itself in 1915 to permit trams to pass through. The Tower houses the Red Gate Gallery, one of the prettiest art galleries in Beijing.

Old Beijing Observatory

北京古观象台

MapIII, E4

Tel (010) 65242202

9am—6pm/10 yuan

The Old Beijing Observatory houses an interesting little museum showing numerous photographs, Chinese astronomical treatises, as well as pictures of the great discoverers. The first observatory was built in the 13th century under the reign of Kublai Khan, but the building you visit dates from the second half of the 15th century. Exposed on the roof are copies of several

instruments for observing and measuring, originals of which can be found in Nanjing. These bronze instruments are remarkable pieces of gold plate, finely worked and decorated. For fans or informed experts, the observatory's internal garden is a most enjoyable place for a rest, sadly lost amongst the traffic of the ring road.

Temple of Wisdom Attained

智化寺

Map III, D3

Tel (010) 65250072

7am—6pm/20 yuan

It houses a pretty pagoda decorated with 10,000 wooden Buddhas in the west. Inside the other pavilions can be found small exhibitions of diverse character: old pottery, collections of phone cards... The last pavilion, Rulai Hall, houses a superb 3 metres high statue of Buddha, surrounded by 9,999 recesses where many Buddhas are deposited, all in different poses. This pavilion

is the most beautiful in the temple, with wooden ceilings of splendidly decorated caissons in red and green. A small corridor on the right gives access to old stairs leading to the floor where three other statues of Buddha stand on lotus flowers. The visit is not that thrilling, but this temple remains one of the most beautiful witnesses to Buddhist architecture during the Ming Dynasty.

Ritan Park

日坛公园

MapIV, B3

Tel (010) 85616301

May—Sept.: 6am—8pm; Oct.—Apr.:

6:30am—8:30pm

Developed in 1530 over an area of more than 20 hectares,

Ritan Park (Temple of the Sun Park) was for a long time the counterpart of the Temple of Heaven Park. Here you can find the same structure, with a gigantic circular altar at the centre, where the Ming and Qing emperors carried out their sacrifices. A large mural depicts the rites of the worship of the sun. The park buildings are in less of a good state than those of the Temple of Heaven and have not been renovated since the development of the Park in the 1950s. This arboretum remains pleasant and elegant. The circular altar is particularly lively: children running in all directions, grown-ups singing or dancing and families meeting up. In the park several attractions for young children (rides, various activities) allow a little time to relax for family groups.

The Temple of the Eastern Peak

东岳庙
MapIV, B3
Tel (010) 65510151
8:30am—4:30pm/Monday closed/10 yuan

This temple, erected in 1319 by a Taoist monk, houses an impressive collection of statues, arranged in themes—justice, vengeance, sickness—in small pavilions set up on the perimeter of the central courtyard. These statues parade a great variety of faces: some entirely human, others half-human, half-animal, others wholly mythological. You can visit the Temple after reading the extraordinary book by the sinologist and explorer Victor Segalen (1878—1919), *China, the Great Statuary* (*Chine, La Grande statuaire*). Numerous Chinese still come to make offerings according to their concerns or wishes at the time. At the centre of the first courtyard stands a forest of steles. A small museum reuniting the beautiful pieces about the history of Beijing has been set up in the last pavilion.

Walking Tour 4:
Around Dongzhimen

There is an east-west axis starting from the Drum Tower and ending at the National Agricultural Exhibition Centre, at the heart of Chaoyang. To the north of this axis are three of Beijing's greatest monuments: the Yonghegong Lama Temple, the Confucius Temple and the Imperial College. The surrounding quarters have been well preserved, and also the visit can conveniently be accompanied by a bicycle ride along the alleyways of the *hutong*. In the eastern half, Dongzhimen Dajie is nicknamed "Ghost Street" or "Caldron Street". Lit by hundreds of red lanterns which swing in the wind all night long (it's one of those rare places in the capital that doesn't close at night), it's a favourite spot for the expats for refined and cheap food at the hundreds of restaurants along the road.

Getting there

Map III, D—E1

This quarter was built up according to a geometric plan with roads at right angles to one another, which makes getting around here much easier than in other quarters. You can get there by the No.107 bus, which leaves from Baishiqiaodong bus station, passes by the Zoo and reaches Dongzhimen via the north gate of Beihai Park. From the south, level with the ancient Ming wall, you can get there by Bus No.24. By underground, get off at Dongzhimen Station.

The Yonghegong Lama Temple

雍和宫
Map III, D1

Tel (010) 64044499
9am—5pm (ticket office closes at 4:30pm)/25 yuan. Audio guide (1hour):20 yuan, available only in Chinese and English.

The largest lamasery in Beijing was rebuilt as the residence of Prince Yong in 1694. When the Prince became Emperor in 1722, his residence was transformed into the Palace of Peace and Harmony, before Emperor Qianlong finally decided in 1744 to make it a lamasery. Over the years this temple acquired great renown and became one of the greatest Tibetan religious centres outside of Tibet. It reopened for religious worship in 1981. Don't forget in the Wanfu Pavilion (the Pavilion of Ten Thousand Happinesses), the imposing monumental statue of Buddha, 24 metres high and sculpted from a

single piece of sandalwood. Just to the left, in the Yansui Pavilion, you can admire an enormous lotus flower, on which sit the Buddha of Longevity. The Lama Temple's Bell Tower houses a very beautiful bell dating from the Ming Dynasty, supported by a bronze dragon.

The entire monument is very well maintained. Don't forget though that it is a place of worship as well as a tourist site. Appropriate dress is expected at all times.

Confucius Temple

孔庙

Map III, D1

Tel (010) 84011977
8:30am—5pm (ticket office closes at 4:30pm)/10 yuan

Leaving the Lama Temple, cross the road and head southwards passing by the shops selling religious artefacts. Take the first road on the right. The Confucius Temple is located 200 metres along. This temple was built in 1302, under the Yuan Dynasty. Originally it formed part of a much larger complex of monuments, including the Imperial College which is situated 100 metres to the west. Of classical design, not least majestic, the Confucius Temple houses 198 stone tablets (steles) engraved with the names of some 52,000 candidates who passed the civil service exams in the imperial court during the Yuan, Ming and Qing dynasties. These steles, erected like an actual forest, can be seen on either side of the entrance inside the temple. In the first courtyard, you can also see an incredible full-size statue of Confucius. In the

Hall of Great Accomplishments (situated within the second courtyard), can be found an exhibition on the life of the master. This hall was first erected in 1302, and then entirely rebuilt in 1411. The interior of the temple itself includes a musical instrument collection. Have a look at the ceiling painted in green and blue shades.

Beyond the temple, in the next courtyard, is a new stele forest, called "The 13 Sutra Table Forest". It concerns an order made by Emperor Kangxi, in 1791, to the calligrapher Jiang Heng. The latter spent 12 years of his life on this monumental piece of work. The tablets recall the works of Confucius and his students. They were renovated in 1988.

On the other side of the courtyard

a small exhibition hall groups together under the name the Capital Museum, several archaeological finds discovered around Beijing. In particular you can find here funereal objects discovered in Han tombs south of Beijing.

Please note that the Confucius Temple completely renovated in 2005. This restoration had become necessary because of the decay to the structure of the buildings.

Imperial College

国子监

Map III, D1
Tel (010)84027224
9am—5pm (ticket office closes at 4:30pm)/20 yuan

Located to the west of the Confucius temple, the Imperial College was at the time of its construction in 1306, the highest national academy in the Yuan Dynasty. It was rebuilt under the Ming, then enlarged and improved in the Qing Dynasty. At the centre of it lies the Biyong Hall (Jade Disc Hall), erected in 1784, where sovereigns came to read and comment upon the writings of Confucius and other great Chinese classics. This hall is particularly notable for its size. The room was built according to a very clever system of wooden pillars and buttresses clearing the way for a vast central space, where the Emperor received at the same time hundreds of young Mandarins, graduates of the examinations.

The square building is surrounded by a canal and an arch bridge. Several dragons decorate the inside of the room where you can see the chair and desk from which the Emperor lectured the students. The room today houses a large collection of drawings and portraits of the great Chinese masters. There you can also see several curious objects. In the gardens and particularly on the central bridge, you will see hundreds of votive tablets tied there by students in the hope of passing their exams. A song and dance performance is held every evening at 7:30pm by the Beijing Opera (from 150 to 580 yuan).

Ditan Park

地坛公园
Map III, C2
Tel (010) 64214657
6am—9pm/2 yuan

Ditan Park (Temple of the Earth Park), was originally a place of sacrifice for the Ming and Qing emperors to their gods of the underworld. It was built in 1530 over 37 hectares. There remains nothing of the original buildings. The majority of the present-day buildings were restored or rebuilt continuously. This park forms one of the axes of the city's cosmic force. It should be considered as one part of a whole which takes in, as well as the Forbidden City, Tiantan Park (Temple of the Heaven Park), where the Temple of Heaven is found and Ritan Park (Temple of the Sun Park).

Walking Tour 5:
South of Qianmen

Chongwen District (崇文区) has maintained a relatively more traditional image. It features a lot of Beijing's grand historical buildings, stretching from the Temple of Heaven Park northwards towards the Drum Tower by way of the Forbidden City and Beihai Lake. Southwest to the Forbidden City is Xuanwu District (宣武区), which offers more insights into Beijing for those who want to explore the city beyond ordinary tourist routes.

The popular *hutong*, close to Qianmen (前门), are gradually being replaced by wide avenues lined with modern tower blocks, consisting of rapidly renovating quarters. The main sites you should remember are Ox Street Mosque (牛街清真寺), at the heart of the Muslim Hui quarter, and the White Cloud Temple (白云观).

Getting there

Chongwen District stretches to the southeast of Beijing, between Qianmen and the Temple of Heaven Park. To get to Chongwen, take Bus No.59 from Qianmen. Hemmed in by the Second Ring Road to the south and the east, the Temple of Heaven Park to the east and the Forbidden City to the north, Xuanwu District is centred on Ox Street, where Beijing's Great Mosque (大清真寺) can be found. Only the northeast of the district is served by the underground. From Qianmen Bus No.59 goes to Daguanyuan Park; Bus No.10 goes towards Ox street from the Forbidden City.

Old Legations Quarter

使馆区
Map III, D4

To the southeast of the Forbidden City lies the old Western Legations Quarter, the first of which was that of the Tsar of Russia, built in 1727. At the start of the 19th century, Britain and France also established embassies here, followed soon after by the German.

Today, the embassies have long since moved to Sanlitun and only a few facades of houses in the western style exist, which can be admired by taking a stroll down the Dongjiaomin Alley. The former French Legation (法国使馆) is located at the corner near the crossing of

this alley and Taijichang Jie. You will also note St Michael's Church (圣米厄尔教堂). The Dutch, Russian and Spanish Legations (荷兰、俄国和西班牙使馆) can also be found in this lane, as well as the old French hospital and the old French post office. If you turn into Taijichang Jie, level with the French Legation, you can find there the facade of the Italian Legation (意大利使馆), without a doubt the most admirable of all.

Natural History Museum

自然博物馆
Map I, D3
Tel (010) 67024431
8:30am—5pm/15 yuan

Situated close to the entrance to the Temple of Heaven, this modern and playful museum is very busy with school groups. Above all it shows itself to be interesting for those who like dinosaur skeletons, for it houses some of the biggest and most complete specimens on display in the world.

The Human Race gallery opens into a magnificent example of a Neanderthal man statue, created during the great era of communist representation. The first floor, dedicated to the Animal Kingdom, presents many photographs and it is above all an impressive gallery of stuffed animals. The effect is striking and children, everywhere you look at this location, are major visitors to this museum.

The Temple of Heaven Park

天坛

Map I, D3

Tel (010) 67028866

8am—5pm/in summer the park
remains open for 1 further hour/35
yuan

Begin your visit early in the morning, strolling along the park's alleyways: it's one of the preferred spots for Beijingers to do their physical exercises.

The Temple of Heaven Park covers an area of 270 hectares to the south of Tian'anmen Square, almost the size of the Summer Palace and twice that of the Forbidden City. The temple was built during the Ming Dynasty in 1420, and underwent great reconstruction work in 1740 and again in 1890 in the Qing Dynasty. This exalted place of worship became, along with the Forbidden City, one of the symbols of Beijing and one of the largest tourist venues in the city.

The starting point for the visit is the vast Round Altar (圆丘坛) (5 metres high), in the south of the park, where the emperors came twice a year, at Winter Solstice and at the first full moon in January to offer sacrifices in the presence of his ministers and government dignitaries. The circular form represents the Heaven, and the square wall surrounding it, the Earth. Thus the emperors always went from the Earth to the Heaven to offer sacrifices. The whole construction was built on the same geometric model of a circle inside a square. You get to the Round Altar by climbing three terraces in succession and a series of nine steps.

The number 9, a symbol of perfection and longevity, can be found in several of the building's details. You can also see nine caldrons to burn the incense, distributed around the ring.

On the Round Altar there are also 360 balustrades, which symbolise the 360 days of the lunar calendar and the 360 degrees of the compass. Finally the numbers of slabs which make up the floor of the circular rings are 9 for the first ring, 18 for the second, 81 for the ninth... In the decorative sculptures you can make out other symbols such as the dragon, representation of the emperor, but equally of the *yang*, and the phoenix, symbol of the empress and of the *yin*.

North to the Round Altar can be found the Echo Wall (回音壁), around 65 metres in diameter, which projects at the centre of the park, the Imperial Vault of Heaven (皇穹宇). The density of

visitors renders the experience almost impossible, but if you get there at a time when there are fewer people, try to whisper at one point on the wall: a person standing on the opposite side of the circle can hear your whisper perfectly, thrown back by the echo. The Imperial Vault of Heaven is a small circular temple where prayer tablets used in the winter solstice ceremony are kept.

Further north still, linked to the Imperial Vault of Heaven by a wide flagstone alleyway is the Hall of Prayer for Good Harvests (祈年殿), the largest of all the buildings. It's a circular temple, 38 metres high and 30 metres in diameter, erected in 1420 at the top of three marble decorated terraces with finely sculptured ramps of imperial and divine symbols. The number 3 can be found in the triple blue tiled roof. Destroyed by fire in 1889, it was soon rebuilt identically.

Beijing Museum of Ancient Architecture

北京古建筑博物馆

Map I, D4

Tel (010) 63045608

9am—4pm/15 yuan

This precious museum set up on quite a large site is located to the west of the Temple of Heaven Park. It reveals itself to be very interesting, in particular the final two halls at the back, one dedicated to housing, and the other to temple architecture, monasteries and lamaseries. The first hall shows traditional construction methods employed in China from their origins. Lovers of cabinet making, joinery and carpentry will take great pleasure in admiring the excellent wooden models illustrating traditional construction techniques. In the last hall is a 1:1,000 scale model of Beijing in 1949.

In the southwest corner of the museum, you can take a few steps between the walls of the Altar of God of Agriculture (先农坛), built in 1420 during the Ming Dynasty, and a place where emperors came to offer sacrifices.

The different objects exhibited in display cases (models, wooden examples of buildings, architectural or ornamental pieces) as well as in the inner courtyard (sculptures, architectural structures) are particularly refined and give

WALKING TOURS

a clear idea of what Beijing's palaces were like right up to the last century.

The Underground City

地下城

Map III, D4
Tel (010) 67022657
8:30am—6pm/20 yuan

Follow Qianmen Dongdajie towards the east as far as its junction with Qinian Dajie. Go down the latter and branch off to the second alley on the right. Walk for 300 metres: the entrance to the underground city is located at No. 62, on the left, Xidamo Changjie.

Between 1969 and 1979, the government undertook the construction of an underground city aimed at protecting the residents of Beijing. About 10 metres or so underground, taking over six years, an enormous complex of underground tunnels was put into place, with a cinema, hospitals, armouries...

The section that can be visited could accommodate up to 300,000 people: the whole network would have been able to welcome 5 million people. One of the underground tunnels links Beijing to Tianjin. A visit to the complex is an amusing experience. You wander for a few minutes underground admiring a few old posters from the Cold War period, before emerging into a vast hall transformed into souvenir shops.

Source of Law Temple

法源寺

Tel (010) 63533772
8:30am—4pm/Closed Wednesday/5 yuan

This temple, built in the 7th century under the Tang Dynasty, displays, in the Hall of Celestial Kings (天王殿), numerous bronze statues dating from the Ming Dynasty when it was rebuilt. The main hall has maintained its admirable architecture. It houses a drum and a bell, as well as an imposing statue of Buddha, in bronze, dating from the Qing Dynasty. In the last hall, don't miss a magnificent statue from the Ming Dynasty representing the Future Buddha (未来佛), seated upon four Buddhas directed towards the compass points, all resting on a stone plinth decorated with 10,000 Buddhas. Today the temple hosts the China Buddhism College and you will come across many students.

Ox Street Mosque

牛街清真寺

Map II, B3
Tel (010) 63532564
6am—7pm/10 yuan/2 yuan for Muslims

The mosque buildings, the oldest in Beijing, first erected at the end of the 10th century, then rebuilt

in the 13th century, like those of the Great Mosque in Xi'an, displays a totally Chinese style of architecture, making it difficult to differentiate, at first glance, from a Taoist temple. However, the arrangements of the buildings and their functions, as well as architectural details reveal all the power and finesse of Chinese Islam. One curiously notes Arab writing drawn with a Chinese brush, an unexpected marriage of two great artistic traditions. The interior of the Mosque can be visited, but the prayer hall is closed to non-Muslims. Appropriate dress is expected.

The most interesting aspect of this visit is the distinctive atmosphere that reigns over and around the Mosque. Chinese Muslims who come here, many originally from Xinjiang, have a very marked physical appearance, quite different from the Han people. They alternate between Arabic and Chinese at ease, or even a local dialect. It's not rare to see groups of people just arrived from the west of China, dressed in traditional costumes, exchanging or selling amazing clothing accessories. In the streets nearby, you can see the permanent nature, right in the heart of Beijing, of a very old rural village culture. The small businesses are still many.

Baoguo Temple

报国寺
Map II, B3
Tel (010) 63173169
7am—4:30pm/Free entry

From Ox Street Mosque, go back up the street to the crossroads with Guang'anmen Jie to the north, then branch off to the left. The temple is on the north side of the road, northbound and 300 metres from the crossroads.

This temple was built in the 12th century and has been for several years invested in by second-hand dealers. You'll find many antiques by strolling along the inner courtyards or even in the streets leading to the temple or surrounding it. As to the halls, they are closed to the public and not visited.

Temple of Heavenly Peace

天宁寺
Map II, B3
9am—4:30pm/opening times liable
to change according to construction
work/prices not available

After leaving Baoguo Temple, going back up you will see the pagoda next to a factory chimney. Turn left when you see it, just before a pedestrian underpass. Its tall octagonal 13-storey structure dates from the 10th century.

White Cloud Temple

白云观
Map II, B3
Tel (010) 63443666
8:30am—4pm/10 yuan

Built in the 8th century, the White Cloud Temple has for a long time been the centre of Taoism in northern China. Passing the first doorway with its three porches symbolising the three worlds of Taoism, visitors finds themselves opposite stone tablets bearing the names of many donors who rendered possible the entire renovation in 1993. The majority of buildings date from the 18th century. The first hall is dedicated to Wang Lingguan, the protector of the Jade Emperor's Palaces. His wooden statue dating from the Ming Dynasty over a soberly decorated room. The Drum and Bell towers stand in the second courtyard, to the east of which is a hall dedicated to three kings: water, heaven and earth.

At the end of the courtyard stands the Jade Emperor's Hall, the most powerful and respected of Taoist deities. The temple dates from 1483, but was rebuilt twice, in 1662 and in 1988. The statue of the Emperor dates from the Ming Dynasty. Religious services take place in the next courtyard, in the Hall of Religious Law (老律堂) which was erected in 1228 and rebuilt in 1456. It was not until the 16th century that the statues of the Seven Immortals were added. The interior is richly decorated in panels, finely sculpted and embellished with gilt.

Walking Tour 6:
West Beijing

Beyond the tourist circuit and well past the little picturesque *hutong* of the city centre, the west of Beijing has some interesting places, which give enough excuses to dive into residential quarters such as those around the White Dagoba Temple (白塔寺).

Getting there

Map II and III
West Beijing covers the districts of Xicheng District (西城区), to the west of the Forbidden City, Haidian District (海淀区), still further west, bordered by the Third Ring Road, and Fengtai District (丰台区), to the south of these two districts. The latter doesn't have much to offer. It's mostly all in a triangle formed by the Purple Bamboo Park (紫竹院公园), Yuyuantan Park (玉渊潭公园) and the White Dagoba Temple where the main interesting sites are to be found: the final two are located close to the underground, whilst the Purple Bamboo Park can be reached by bus 114, 118 206, 211 and so on.

Military Museum

中国军事博物馆
Map II, A3
Tel (010) 66866244
Nov.—March: 8am—5pm/Apr.—Oct.: 8am—5:30pm/ticket office closes 30 minutes before/20 yuan
Interested in the Long March, the

War of Resistance Against Japan, the Revolutionary War, the Cold War and the War to Resist US Aggression and Aid Korea, you will find here the opportunity to perfect their knowledge on these subjects, on the condition of being able to speak Chinese of course. The main objective of the military museum is the preservation of military artefacts covering the country's recent history. It's also an educational museum, designed to teach one a view of the history and enlightenment of the Revolution. On the ground floor, beyond a gigantic statue of Mao,

are exhibited cannons, tanks and aircrafts of different countries, as well as a splendid pair of official cars from the legendary "Red Flag" marque, dating from the 1950's and 1960's.

In the outer courtyard, among aircrafts and boats on display, you note the presence of the wreck of a US U2 spy plane, shot down by the PLA Air Force on 9th September 1962 above eastern China.

The galleries on the floors above retrace the history of the Chinese Army from the War of Resistance Against Japan. Shown in dozens of display cases are hundreds of blades and individual weapons of every kind and from everywhere. An entire room is given to the Long March. The museum has a rich collection related to the Revolution, supplemented by models and statues in the purest realist style.

Millennium Monument

中华世纪坛
Map II, A2

Tel (010) 68573281
www.bj2000.org.cn
8am—6pm/ticket office closes 45 minutes
before/30 yuan

Directly behind the Military Museum stands the huge Millennium Monument which presents itself like a gigantic sundial. In the main hall you see a vault held up by 8 gilded columns surrounding one huge pylon. All around, frescos illustrate the finest hours in China's history. Outside on a stage another fresco depicts the 56 ethnic groups in China. The Millennium Monument organises regular exhibitions dedicated to Chinese and foreign artists.

Capital Museum

首都博物馆

Map II, B3

Tel (010) 63370491

www.capitalmuseum.org.cn

www.beijingmuseum.org.cn

9am—4pm/Closed Mon./50 yuan

This new museum, opened in 2006, impresses first with its monumental and innovative architecture: architects Jean-Marie Duthilleul and Cui Kai have devised, behind the glass, stone and bronze façade which reprises certain traditional Chinese elements, a vast engraved bronze cylinder which faces a cube containing the exhibition halls. The museum tells the story of Beijing, its culture and how it was built, through a variety of objects and reconstructions of streets and scenes from daily

life. The collections of works of art, calligraphy, bronze, jade, sculpture and china, all beautiful objects, are exhibited with meticulous museology, worthy of international standards. It is a good place for vistors to get a taste of classical Chinese art in all its forms of expression.

On the digital tour, free computers allow you to observe in detail paintings and calligraphy displayed with enlightening commentaries. The galleries on the ground floor and first floor welcome contemporary quality exhibitions coming from overseas museums (Egyptian art, Indian art…).

Yuyuantan Park

玉渊潭公园

Map II, A2

6am—9:30pm/till10:30pm from June to Sept/2 yuan

This little park is very popular with families from the nearby residential areas, who meet here in summer evenings or at weekends for picnics around the great central pool. On this

site there once stood a palace of which nothing remains, apart from the lake which passed through it and on which you can take a boat ride. Not to miss the cherry blossom which is the most beautiful scenery in spring.

Purple Bamboo Park

紫竹院公园

Map II, A1

6am—8pm/till 9pm in summer/2 yuan/1 yuan extra for a visit to the bamboo forest.

This tiny but charming park was first landscaped under the Qing, to the northeast of today's park. With three lakes, more than a third of the surface area is covered in water, which makes this a superb oasis of cool air during the hot hours of summer days. Several types of bamboo are maintained here. The atmosphere here is particularly calm and serene compared with other city parks and many chess players come here to play.

Beijing Art Museum (The Temple of Longevify)

北京艺术博物馆（万寿寺）

Map II, A1

Tel (010) 68413380/66161141

9am—4pm/60 yuan.

The Temple of Longevify, erected during the Ming Dynasty in 1577, is known in Beijing as a mini-Forbidden City. The classical entrance with bell and drum towers opens onto the same red walls and gilded roofs as those of the Forbidden City. In fact, after the enlargement of the temple by Emperor Qianlong in 1761, the successing emperors began the habit of stopping here on the way to the Summer Palace.

The Drum Tower houses a small exhibition on the history of the site. The temple originally housed a collection of Buddhist scriptures in Chinese. The first construction covered an area of almost 65 hectares, linked to the Forbidden City by the Changhe canal. This continued on in the Summer Palace, in the northwest of Beijing. The temple bell, which weighed 46.5 tons, was moved to another temple in the northwest of the city. It was covered in more than 230,000 Sanskrit and Chinese characters.

The halls and the wings of the temple now house an interesting art gallery (艺术博物馆), comprising a rich collection of china and jade crockery from different periods. Almost all the notices are translated into English!

At the back of the final courtyard is a stone forest behind which stands the Temple of Buddha Eternal (无量寿佛殿), dating from 1761. The statue of Buddha was unfortunately stolen and replaced by a small pagoda. Look at the ceilings which have been superbly carved.

Five-Pagoda Temple

五塔寺

Map II, A1

Tel (010) 62173543

9am—4pm/Every day exc. Mon./20 yuan,free entry Weds

To reach this charming little temple, go along the canal on the north bank towards the east from the Purple Bamboo Park. Pass the skating rink and you'll pick out the temple on the left thanks to its five pagodas.

The five pagodas are all that remain of a temple erected by Emperor Chengzu of the Ming Dynasty in the 15th century and destroyed in 1927. The entrance, on the right, leads to a forest of steles, which is very beautiful and very well sculpted. The temple houses more than a thousand of these stone tablets, some of which date from the Tang Dynasty. On the left, on the opposite side of the forest of steles, you can see numerous statues taken from various tombs across the country: dignitaries and mythical creatures like those along the Spirit Way to the Ming tombs. These animals placed on either side of a passageway leading to a tomb mark the status of the person buried there. Several doors to tombs and vaults are also kept here, as well as another forest of steles. Among these stand stone funeral tablets in the northwest corner, which tell of the work of Jesuits who came to China during the Ming and Qing dynasties. Behind you will find several discrete bas-relief sculptures and carved Buddhas.

At the back of the temple a very interesting exhibition on the techniques of stone carving calligraphy allows you to better understand how it has developed over the centuries. Notices are translated into English and the museum shows photographs of many of the carved animals.

At the centre, the vast building supporting the five pagodas is made entirely from marble of admirable quality. The interior gives an exhibition on the history of the different stages of renovation of this temple, in Chinese only, unfortunately. A narrow staircase leads to the roof. The bas-reliefs of the five square-based pagodas are a masterpiece, but the majority are badly damaged.

Lu Xun Museum

鲁迅博物馆

Map III, A3

Tel (010) 66165654

9am—4pm/5 yuan

From the Fuchengmen underground station go back up a hundred meters or so then head towards the east down the little *hutong* after having passed a little park arranged on the pavement and aiming towards the top of

the White Dagoba Temple, the museum can be found 200 metres on the left.

This museum dedicated to the writer Lu Xun is arranged around a lovely exhibition hall where drawings, writings and photographs are brought together. On the left of the museum is the former residence of Lu Xun, old buildings spreading about a central courtyard where many personal items of the master have been preserved. You can look inside through the windows and thus discover the writer's surroundings. Note the great asceticism of the place. A single building is open to visitors. At the exit you'll find a bookshop, well stocked with Lu Xun's major works and some calligraphy. Almost all the books have been translated into English.

The White Dagoba Temple

白塔寺

Map III, A3

Tel (010) 66160211

8am—5pm/10 yuan

After leaving the Lu Xun Museum, you can choose to lose yourself for a while in the *hutong* which can be found between two buildings, or just go directly to Fuchengmennei Dajie, to the south, where the entrance to the temple is found.

The great stupa of the White Dagoba Temple was erected

in 1271 in the reign of Kublai Khan. From the following year onwards, a temple was built around the dagoba. History has it that in order to determine the boundaries of the temple, Kublai Khan fired four arrows in the direction of the four points of the compass. The walls were built between the points where the arrows landed. Destroyed by successive fires, the temple was rebuilt in 1344 and again in 1457. During the Qing Dynasty, it was enlarged in 1668 and again in 1753. Profiting from these latter construction works, Emperor Qianlong had hidden several relics and Buddhist manuscripts in the stupa so as to protect them from potential invaders. In 1976, the stupa was badly damaged in an earthquake. It was not until 1978, during the renovation work, that these manuscripts were discovered by labourers. You will see that the two lions marking the entrance to the temple have curiously been reversed: the lion holding the cub under its paw is on the right, whilst the lion holding the ball is on the left. The interior of the temple houses a pretty museum whose notices are translated into English. The end point of the visit is the magnificent collection of Buddhist figurines and statues. In this temple a sober and serene atmosphere reigns, which is favourable to meditation.

Temple of Ancient Monarchs

历代帝王庙
Map III, A3
Tel (010) 66530060
9am—4pm/20 yuan

Situated 200 metres to the east of the White Dagoba Temple on Fuchengmennei Dajie, the Temple of Ancient Monarchs in China, very seldomly visited by tourists, has been recently renovated. It was built in 1530 to honour the memory of the glorious ancestors of all Chinese dynasties. The new buildings line up, with flashy paintwork, red doors and yellow or green glazed roof tiles, and they are interspersed with various courtyards, where many stone tablets stand. The characters engraved on them are unfortunately almost all erased. The mythical carved creatures which hold up the stone tablets are by contrast admirable.

The Hall of Saint Worship (崇圣殿), supported by 60 red columns consists of splendid painted ceilings. It unfortunately looks a bit too modern and insipid, but the low historical interest is compensated for by the elegance of the temples and the small amount of visitors.

The Temple of Great Charity

广济寺

Map III, B3

Tel (010) 66160907

8am—4:30pm/Free entry

This peaceful and calm temple houses several steles to admire in the coolness of its shaded courtyard. The architecture is very classical, though the construction of the temple goes back to the 12th century. It was rebuilt once under the Ming, then in New China after having been destroyed by fire. The temple remains a place of worship and offerings: be careful not to disturb the prayers and worshippers.

Walking Tour 7 :
Around Beijing

The Summer Palace

颐和园

MapI, B1
Tel (010) 62881144
Apr.—Oct.: 6:30am—8pm/60 yuan
Nov.—March: 7am—7pm/Ticket office
closes 2 hours earlier/50 yuan

Get there from Qianmen by Bus 690; Give yourself one and half an hour for the journey.

Located in the western suburbs of the city, the Summer Palace and the Fragrant Hills Park (香山公园) give you a chance to get away from the bustling scene of the city, though difficult to schedule the two visits in one day. You'll find little stalls for lunch, or shops selling instant noodles. But the best solution is to prepare for yourself a small snack which you can eat in the shade of a pagoda or in the open air, close to an ornamental lake.

In the near suburbs of Beijing, the Summer Palace is not to be missed, above all if you're looking for shade and fresh air. This vast park, totalling 300 hectares and consisting of lakes and gardens, was developed in the northwest of Beijing by Emperor Yongzheng to allow him to leave the over-hot atmosphere of the Forbidden City on summer days. Its current scale is a reflection of the huge

works carried out under the orders of Emperor Qianlong in the 18th century and the renovations ordered by Empress Dowager Cixi at the end of the 19th century. Nevertheless, there are few original buildings. After it was set on fire by the Eight-power Allied Forces when they entered Beijing in 1900, it was necessary to restore the entire park, and the actual reconstruction was carried out at the start of the 20th century and above all after 1949.

The bus will drop you off at the east entrance to the palace where you come out at a small labyrinth of palace buildings and interior courtyards before arriving at Kunming Lake (昆明湖) (Lake of Tranquility), which covers three quarters of the surface of the Summer Palace. At the heart of this maze, you'll find the Hall of Benevolence and Longevity (仁寿殿), where the emperor received ministers and dealt with state affairs. The courtyard is decorated with magnificent bronzes of mythical animals.

Just to the north of the Palace is located the most relaxing spot: Garden of Harmonious Virtue (德和园). The vast Kunming Lake, which you can explore by boat or pedalo or even on foot by crossing the 17-Arch Bridge (17孔桥) that links the island to the southern part of the lake, is dominated by Longevity Hill (万寿山) where the Tower of Buddhist Incense (佛香阁) sits imposingly.

The northern shore of the lake is lined with the magnificent Long Corridor (长廊), 700 metres long and decorated with numerous scenes in Chinese history. On the west side, you can find the

Marble Boat (石舫) which the Empress Dowager Cixi had it built to host dinner parties in the lake's cool air.

Crossing the bridge behind the boat, towards the small western island, you'll find a small exhibition hall showing artists and calligrapher's works. From there climb the hill towards the Tower of Buddhist Incense and the Sea of Wisdom Temple (智慧海), covered in glazed tiles and walls decorated with little Buddha. The view over the lake is magnificent. Going back down towards the Jingfu Pavilion (景福阁), to the east will get you back to the entrance.

If you go to Beijing in winter, give yourself a half day to visit the Summer Palace and anticipate warm clothing to go skating on Kunming Lake in the company of Beijingers.

Yuanmingyuan

圆明园

Tel (010) 62628501
7am—7pm/10 yuan for the park, 15 yuan extra for access to the ruins
Seventeen kilometres east of the Summer Palace. Go from Xizhimen underground station by Bus No. 365.

Less well-known than the Summer Palace, Yuanmingyuan is, however, worth the detour. It was started in 1709 under Emperor Kangxi, and all together took 151 years to finish. The area, a magnificent blending of the best in Western and Chinese architecture, was nicknamed "the Versailles of the Orient" up until its destruction by the Anglo-French force when it sacked the Summer Palace in 1860. Today existing only as a collection of

making the climb up the hill, you can visit the Temple of the Azure Clouds (碧云寺), built during the Yuan Dynasty in 1331. With its magnificent stupa reaching 35 metres high, on the side of the hill, it offers an absolutely magnificent view, as much of the Western Hills in the south as of Beijing itself.

Finally, follow the path which leads to the Incense Burner Peak (香炉峰), the summit of the Park. The whole thing has been well developed and constitutes a pleasant walk of about one hour for the climb amongst floral paths, discovering temples and pagodas. At the summit, the panorama is often spoiled by the mist. But in winter, or during windy and clear days, you can take in Beijing, a city as large as the whole of Belgium, in a blink of the eye. You can prolong the walk towards Mount Shou'an (寿安山) and the Sleeping Buddha Temple (卧佛寺). The descent takes about 30 minutes. You'll have no problem finding a taxi to get back to the city.

majestic ruins, it is still a popular site for both Chinese and foreign visitors. A small museum at the entrance to the park exhibits the drawings showing the palace before its destruction.

Fragrant Hills Park

香山公园
MapI, A1
Tel (010) 62591264
Park: 6am—6:30pm,7pm in summer/10 yuan
Temple of the Azure Clouds: 8am—4pm, 4:30pm in summer/10 yuan
rope way to Incense Burner Peak: 50 yuan during the week, 60 yuan weekends and holidays.

Located to the northwest of the Summer Palace, the Fragrant Hills Park was another place to relax for the emperors. Arriving at the main gate to the north, before

Walking Tour 8:
The Great Wall and the Imperial Tombs

It's impossible to imagine a visit to Beijing without a trip to the Great Wall. A simple peek at the greatest man-made structure or a much longer hike over the many thousands of stones: Beijing's surroundings are rich in trips of this kind. Six departure points will let you find one you like, depending on how much time you have and how well you can walk.

Getting there and back

The simplest solution consists of choosing the section of the Wall that you'd like to visit and join a group. Generally speaking all youth hostels and tourist hotels in Beijing organise trips to the main locations, Badaling being the most frequently offered. You can also make your own transport arrangements locally, even if that requires a little patience for some destinations like Huanghuacheng.

Some bearings

From Beijing, Badaling (八达岭): 70km (northwest); Juyongguan (居庸关): 50km (northwest); Mutianyu (慕田峪): 100km (north); Huanghuacheng (黄花城): 60km (north); Simatai (司马台): 110km (northeast); Jinshanling (金山岭): 110km (northeast).

Advice

Take provisions with you, especially water in summer, but travel light: the climbs can be long! Take advantage of the lovely winter days to avoid the crowds and enjoy the Wall covered in snow. Either way, a good pair of walking shoes is more than recommended.

▶ By organised tour

Local operators organise daily trips to different sections of the Great Wall. In Beijing you'll find buses to Badaling east of Qianmen (前门) and tours all over Tian'anmen Square (天安门广场). The fare is 50 yuan per person and doesn't include entry to the site. A trip to Badaling is almost always accompanied by a visit to the Ming Tombs, between Beijing and Badaling. For Mutianyu, operators are located at Dozhimen (东直门) station. Reckon on 60 yuan per person return. The same tariff and departure point applies for Simatai.

▶ By local transport

For Badaling, take Bus No. 919 from Deshengmen (德胜门). Give yourself 2 hours for the journey. More modern buses can do the trip in just 1 hour, but cost twice as much. Tourist buses also available from Qianmen (Bus No.1) and the central station (北京站) (Bus No. 2). The last buses leave Badaling for Beijing between 6:30pm and 7pm, a little later in high season when Badaling stays open until 8pm. The same buses go to Juyongguan Pass, but be careful not to get on a non-stopping service. Let the driver know you want to get off at Juyongguan. For Mutianyu, leave from the long distance bus station at Dongzhimen by Bus No. 916 or 936. Reckon on 90 minutes journey time. These buses do not operate a regular service, and you could equally as well get one of the many buses for Huairou (怀柔) District where minibuses will wait for you till the end of the journey. Another bus for Mutianyu: Bus No. 6 departs from Xuanwumen (weekends and holidays only).

For Huanghuacheng, also leave from Dongzhimen by Bus No. 961 as far as Huanghuacheng village, or by Bus No. 916 as far as Huairou then take a minibus as far as Huanghuacheng. The last buses leave Huanghuacheng around 5pm. For Simatai, there are many buses in the morning, still from Dongzhimen. Allow 90 minutes and 20 yuan for the trip. For Jinshanling, take the same route.

You can also choose to go by minibus to Miyun (密云) County, where other minibuses will then take you to the Wall at Simatai, Jinshanling or Huanghuacheng. Buses for Chengde can also make a stop at Simatai or Jinshanling, as long as you let the driver know. A taxi or minibus will take you to your final destination.

▶ By taxi

This is perhaps the most costly option, but you can agree upon a route to see various sections of the Wall quickly. It's particularly suitable for family groups with young children. Negotiate a price first and don't pay until you get back to Beijing. Only agree to fuel on the way back, not in advance, and make it clear where you want to go: if the driver decides to use the motorway to get to Badaling or Simatai, it's very unlikely he'll pay the toll out of his own pocket. Excluding motorway tolls, entrance fees, food and lodging, a taxi for three days for a trip between the six locations listed above shouldn't cost more than 1,500 yuan, divided by the number of passengers in the car.

At Badaling, you can find an ATM accepting Visa cards. Everywhere else have some cash on you.

WALKING TOURS

Where to stay

You can find, close to the main sites, somewhere to stay and eat. Obviously, at the most touristy spots like Badaling or Juyongguan Pass, prices are the highest. However, as these sites are very close to Beijing we'd recommend you going there in a day or passing by a hotel in Beijing who could perhaps offer you good rates with a local partner hotel. For locations further away from Beijing a night on site is perfectly reasonable– even recommended – and you can find somewhere to stay on a modest budget without great difficulty.

At Huanghuacheng

▶ *Xiaohong's Hostel*

晓红一路发

Tel (010) 61651393

E-mail: damatthewall@ hotmail.com

In the village, look out for the sign Xiaohong's Hostel, on the left on the high street. A double room costs 105 yuan and there are 40 beds in a dormitory for 10 to 35 yuan depending on the level of comfort. The cheapest dormitories are very spartan: a single plank covering half the room on which guests cram in side by side, under the bedclothes. The shared bathrooms are basic. This small establishment remains open all year round and the welcome couldn't be any warmer. The location is perfect for starting a complete tour of Huanghuacheng early in the morning. The team also provides food: plentiful dishes, and a good price-quality ratio.

▶ *Jintang Villa*

金汤山庄

Tel (010) 61651134

63 rooms from 298 to 890 yuan depending on the category and time of the year/ Breakfast: 20 yuan

Situated on the side of the lake between the two sections of the Wall around Huanghuacheng, this establishment is perfect for those who want to sleep at the foot of the Wall. However, it's a bit old, very over-priced and the location less convenient since you are forced to leave in one direction or the other, and then retrace your steps.

At Simatai

▶ *Sima Restaurant & Hotel*

司马台长城国际青年旅社

Tel 69035311/13701265674

Open all year round. Ideal for staying at the foot of the most impressive part of the Wall whose shadow is cast on the summit of the steep mountains on the other side of the lake which adjoins the inn. Well equipped comfortable rooms available for 260 yuan or a place in the dorm for 50 yuan a bed. This establishment possesses a high priced restaurant, but a reasonable one with regards to quantity, and a pleasant terrace on the lakeside.

At Jinshanling

▶ *Jinshan Hotel*
100m on the right after entering the site.

金山宾馆
Tel (0314) 8830479
10 rooms and dorms
Closed from Nov. to Apr.
Very well located for those wanting to set off on a hike early to Simatai, this basic but clean hotel offers double rooms for 160 yuan and rooms with five beds for 320 yuan. When busy the slightly older rooms are put back into use. Altogether a bit over-priced, but the staff are very nice and the atmosphere less touristy than elsewhere.

At Badaling

▶ *Commune by the Great Wall—Kempinski Hotels*
长城脚下的公社 凯宾斯基饭店
Tel (010) 81181888
www.commune.com.cn and www.kempinski.com.
Take a bus to Badaling, then a minibus as far as the section at Shuiguan. By taxi, take the Shuiguan exit on the motorway, and then follow the signs. The ancient and the modern, wild nature and sophistication side by side in an altogether architecturally bold building, a couple of steps from the Great Wall: 11 villas for hire by the night (6 to 10 people) and a restaurant, designed by Asian architects.

This place which absolutely cannot be categorised is a veritable modern art gallery with an open roof, which you can visit for 120 yuan. Booking is mandatory.

Where to eat

All the places listed above offer food. You'll find as well, adjacent to all the sites, many other restaurants and shops selling instant noodles.

The prices naturally are high compared to the amount and quality. A good solution is to bring your own snacks and stop for a picnic in some peaceful spot on the Wall.

When to visit the Wall?

For hiking, come in autumn, when the leaves lend the scenery a whole range of colours and different parts of the Wall are safely accessible. But, for the simple beauty of the structure, and as long as you are willing to confine yourself to the vicinity of the sites which are open without taking long walks, winter is unquestionably the most beautiful season, when the blue sky dominates a countryside covered in snow and when the ice forms ephemeral sculptures on the trees and bushes which litter the steps and watchtowers. Besides, it's much less busy when it's freezing. Consider warm clothing, something to change into after walking and shoes that grip well.

History

The Great Wall has the same effect on tourists as moths to a flame. Who has never dreamt of walking along it? The Great Wall of China runs for over 5,000 kilometre, from the Yellow Sea as far as the Marches of the Gobi desert. To the west can be found ruins around Dunhuang, in Gansu. However, it is in the east, around Beijing that large sections have been sufficiently well preserved and even in some cases, restored over the course of the last fifty years.

▶ *A project of gigantic proportions*

Construction of this colossal structure began in the 7th century BC. At the time it was simply a few small walls, built by local warlords and served as the martial recovery engineering system of the different places and nations. It wasn't until 220 BC that the First Emperor of China, also the first sovereign to have unified the country under one law, decided to protect the whole of his Empire with a gigantic line of fortifications. The construction of 15,000 towers and 25,000 forts, as well as the steps and walls which linked them required the mobilisation of thousands of soldiers, peasants and prisoners from the whole empire. It is at Simatai, where the Wall stands upon the crest of the mountains that you realise how enormous the project was.

WALKING TOURS

The Great Wall 长城

Badaling

八达岭

Tel (010) 69121226
Summer: 6:30am—7pm; Winter:
7am—6pm/45 yuan including access
to the Wall and museum cable car: 60
yuan return

The busiest of the restored sections of the Great Wall is located 70 kilometres from Beijing. And for those who don't have a lot of time, it's the most practical destination. If you organise yourself well, half a day is enough to visit Badaling. Several kilometres of wall have been restored here, once in the 1950's, then again in the 1980's. It has all been arranged for mass tourism, from coach parks to dressing up for souvenir photos. The density of visitors there in high season is comparable to passengers on the underground and you have to stand shoulder to shoulder to find your way up the steps. The majority of tourists head north; the southern part is in fact relatively less crowded. Unfortunately, the walk ends quickly, limited to the restored parts. The rest are so badly damaged that the trip can be fraught with danger. Suffice to say Badaling offers one of the most beautiful views on the Great Wall whose watch towers and steps follow the contours of the surrounding hills. The site is absolutely wonderful in winter, when the crowd is less dense and the snow covers the walls.

A small cable-car allows you to effortlessly reach the panoramic viewpoint. Crawling up is however less hard than at Simatai. The village which spreads out at the foot of the Wall consists essentially of souvenir shops. You'll find absolutely any gadget, T-shirt, pin or baseball hat you can get hold of. Further away there is also a zoo. The museum on the other hand, as long as you can still stand the crowds, offers a quarter hour documentary on the history of the Great Wall, as well as scale models allowing you to understand in detail the construction techniques used. Several photographs show different parts of the Great Wall in other Chinese provinces.

Juyongguan Pass

居庸关

Tel (010) 69771665
8am—5pm/45 yuan, free for children
under 1.20 metres

Just as busy as Badaling, but in a less spectacular setting, this section of the Wall has been renovated recently. You are able to see the buildings which marked the passage towards the capital. It is nearer to Beijing than Badaling and, if you are short of time, this would be your best choice. Juyongguan Pass is only 50 kilometres northwest of Beijing.

Mutianyu

慕田峪长城
Tel (010) 61626022
7am—6:30pm/40 yuan cable-car: 50 yuan return

About a hundred kilometres northeast of Beijing, Mutianyu is a good compromise between accessibility and crowds of tourists. The panorama is not as wonderful as Badaling, but impressive nonetheless. The wall has been renewed here over a little more than 2 kilometres which you can walk along, much more calmly than at Badaling. The large numbers of bastions and watchtowers make the site even more beautiful in winter and give you some shade in summer. Besides, the souvenir seller is mildly less than at Badaling, once passed the line of shops at the entrance.

WALKING TOURS

The walk to the summit is easy, but long. A cable-car gets you to the highest point from where you can come back down to Mutianyu or even go further towards the less touristy and un-restored parts, in the direction of Huanghuacheng.

Huanghuacheng

黄花城长城
Tel (010) 61651111
7:30am—5:30pm/25 yuan

Huanghuacheng is the best bet for anyone wanting to go off the beaten track and put their feet on the real unspoilt Great Wall. Of course the views are not as impressive as at Simatai or Mutianyu, but do not diminish the surroundings of a magnificent walk along the greatest man-made structure ever built. The other advantage of Huanghuacheng is that it permits several walks to be done, depending on what you want and your level of fitness. Finally, it's also the starting point to the most well-known sections of the Wall: from Huanghuacheng, you can reach Badaling towards the west in seven days by foot, and then Mutianyu to the east in about four days.

The wall goes from east to west from one part of the village to the other. You can make a complete loop, or cut the route into two by choosing one side or the other. To make a complete loop north of Huanghuacheng Village, count on 4 to 5 hours' walking. Leaving the village, pass under the sign "Tiange Pick

Paradise", a little further on from Sanjia Warehouse, and follow the main path, which runs along a cemetery then a canal, as far as the somewhat chinglish signboard forbidding access to the Wall. The first few hundred meters have been restored, but afterwards the Wall is in its original state. Follow the Wall towards the west. You'll reach the first lake, almost halfway along the route, where some stalls offering you the chance to buy something to eat. The climb down to the lake and the climb back up the other side are subject to an entry fee, but there is no gate to stop you from entering if you get there early. The tarmac road reaches the lake and cuts the Wall into two; it takes you directly towards Huanghuacheng if you decide to cut the walk into two.

Continuing towards the west, the second part of the walk is more difficult. The Wall is in a bad state, often blocked by prickly bushes, and the watchtowers often have to be bypassed or climbed. The climb down to the second lake is almost impossible by following the line of the Wall and in order to finish you have to take the narrow paths along the sides of the hills. Follow the main road towards Huanghuacheng via Zhuangdaokou Village (撞道口村).

Simatai

司马台长城

Tel (010) 69031051

5am—5pm, 7pm in summer/40 yuan

Simatai is the furthest part of the wall from Beijing, and also the most beautiful and the most gripping. The distance from Beijing means it is relatively less busy. Located 110 kilometres north east of Beijing, near to Gubeikou (古北口) Village, this large section of wall perfectly demonstrates the difficulties engineers and labourers must have faced in order to build the Wall in extreme conditions. Perched upon the crest of the mountains, and in some places exceeding a gradient of 60 degrees, the steps link towers which look down on bottomless ravines. It is without doubt the most impressive section of the Wall. If going up or coming down scares you, take the cable-car: it

offers you, without risk or effort, the chance to see the magnificent views. If you are on foot, take something to drink and some sturdy shoes. The steps are often very high and you'll often need to call upon all four limbs to clamber up. The way down can be made by flying over the lake below, via a cable and harness, 35 yuan, if you are tempted by adventure!

Jinshanling

金山岭
Tel (0314) 8830222
7am—5pm/50 yuan

Close to Simatai, a site you can reach on foot in just a few hours, this section of the Wall has the advantage of being still broadly walkable and relatively less busy, without having been greatly renovated. The level of difficulty can be classed as "relaxing", even if certain

paths are tricky: that allows you to benefit fully from the views. Jinshanling combines the countryside's authenticity and beauty which, without attaining Simatai's magnificence, is no less imposing for it, as soon as you have cleared the 25 watchtowers. Less busy a few years ago, the site has more recently regained interest, attracting a growing number of hikers hoping to practice. Although you can walk here all the year round, the un-renovated sections remain passable with difficulty and are very dangerous in winter.

It's possible to reach Simatai by foot from Jinshanling. This superb hike organised by many hotels from Beijing and made more and more by visitors, lets you see two of the most beautiful places on the Great Wall of China all by wandering off the beaten track.

Leaving early in the morning from Jinshanling, you can easily cover 10 kilometres to Simatai before noon. The level of difficulty is not high, but some parts of the Wall have not been renovated and require a good level of physical fitness. Reckon on a pace of about 2.5 to 3 kilometres/hour. Arriving at Simatai, you have to buy a ticket to enter the site and then pay for the right to go across the footbridge which joins the two sections of the Wall. If you aren't too tired you can tackle the climb up Simatai: that alone will require the same effort as the 10 kilometres you have just covered.

Hiking on the Great Wall

If you plan on taking an excursion of several days along the wall, be aware that it is extremely dangerous and that it requires a high level of physical fitness. Without weighing yourself down too much, you must take with you sufficient water and provisions. Good shoes are obviously essential as well as a light, solid halyard type rope, to hoist your bags behind you keeping you free to move along the difficult routes. It's recommended to take a mobile phone, useful in case of accidents (they do happen often) on the parts of the Wall that are not supervised. Finally and above all, you are well advised not to go on your own.

Ming Tombs 明十三陵

Halfway between Beijing and the Badaling Great Wall, the Ming Tombs form part of those up to now unmissable tours around the Chinese capital, to such a point that it has become difficult to get there on time. The excursion is almost always combined with a visit to the Wall at Badaling (and vice versa). The highly touristy atmosphere which reigns over it makes the site difficult to appreciate, even though it was chosen and landscaped, at the time of its foundation, according to the rules of *fengshui*.

Getting there and back

▶ Organised Tours

The simplest solution, if you are also planning to visit Badaling the same day, is to join an organised tour. Buses leave in the morning at regular intervals from Qianmen, southeast of Tian'anmen Square (between 6am and 10:30am; reckon on 50 yuan per person). The visit to the Ming Tombs is on the way back.

▶ By local transport

For going just to the Ming Tombs, take Bus No. 345 at Deshengmen. The journey takes 1 hour for less than 10 yuan. Go down to Changping District, where other buses or minibuses will drive you to the site entrance. Almost all of Beijing's hotels organise excursions to the Ming Tombs, combined or not with a trip to Badaling. Ask at your hotel.

▶ By taxi

Reckon on about 200 yuan return, divided by the number of people in the car. Book the taxi with your hotel: you'll save time in the negotiation.

The Ming Dynasty reigned over China between 1368 and 1644. The first Ming emperor was Zhu Yuanzhang, established his capital in Nanjing, but his son Zhu Di later chose to transfer the capital to Beijing. The Ming reign was characterised by its deep return to traditional Chinese values and by a renewal of Confucianism. The height of the regime was quickly reached under Zhu Di, or Emperor Chengzu, but his successors, stretching the boundaries of its politics, ended by rounding China off as a country turned into itself, falling further behind the West. Thirteen of the sixteen Ming emperors who governed China are buried close to the village of Changping. Located in a hollow of a mountainous arc, chosen and commissioned by experts according to *fengshui*, the site is very well restored and the architecture of the tombs is impressive.

Don't fail to visit the museum, located to the right of the entrance to the site. It displays many photographs of the excavations and the restoration, as well as official photographs of political leaders having visited the site. There are also explanatory notices about the different tombs, the only ones on the site.Entry included in the ticket price.

Sacred Way

神路

30 yuan

This 7-kilometre long paved way leads to the Changling Tomb. Named "Sacred Way", it starts under a triumphal arch. It passes by a hall housing China's tallest stone tablet, supported at the base by a dragon-like turtle. It then continues along bordered by sculptures of real and mythical animals and Chinese dignitaries. In total, 12 pairs of animals face one another each side of the way, as well as 12 high ranking officials. The main car park is to be found between the Spirit Way and the Changling Tomb. If you come by taxi, ask the driver to stop at the entrance to the way, otherwise you risk only seeing the statues through the car windows.

Changling Tomb

长陵

8am-5pm/45 yuan in summer, 30 yuan in winter

Changling, the tomb of Emperor Chengzu, the third Ming emperor, was the first vault to be built in the valley. During his reign from 1403 to 1424, he reinforced his father's work and strengthened China's presence on the margins of the empire. His tomb, the largest, at the centre of all, reflects his power and inspired the design of subsequent funeral vaults. It took almost twenty years to bring the construction to an end. Only one part has

WALKING TOURS

been opened up. The climax of the visit is the passageway in the enormous hall of funerary objects.

Dingling Tomb

定陵

8am-5:30pm/65 yuan in summer, 40 yuan in winter

Dingling houses the thirteenth Ming emperor, Zhu Yijun, who reigned from 1572 to 1620. The Ming Dynasty was snuffed out 24 years after Zhu Yijun's death, replaced by the Qing Dynasty. The visit gives an opportunity to admire several pieces of Chinese funereal furniture. The Empress Xiaoduan is interred next to her husband.

Zhaoling Tomb

昭陵

8:30am-4pm/30 yuan in summer, 20 yuan in winter

A bit isolated on this site. Visitors are fewer in number here and the atmosphere less noisy.

Qing Tombs 清陵

Often wrongly neglected, the Qing vaults are located 125 kilometre from Beijing and forty kilometres or so south of Simatai. The distance and the lack of maintenance contribute to the low popularity of the site, particularly out of season. The tombs of Emperors Qianlong and Kangxi or that of the Empress Dowager Cixi are however infinitely more interesting. The view is, moreover, more stunning, with the tombs lining up within the cellars of numerous palaces scattered about this vast valley. There is no set route traced out and you can stroll about at leisure among the different vaults: a trip offering a welcome change of surroundings, outside of the too touristy world of Beijing's outskirts.

Some bearings

125 kilometres northeast of Beijing, in Hebei province.

What not to miss

Several moments of contemplation in front of the frescos on Qianlong's tomb.

Advice

If you go by taxi, be sure your driver knows the route and carry a map with you, just in case.

Getting there and back

▶ *By organised tour*

Tourist buses leave from Beijing at weekends only, from Xuanwumen (宣武门) underground station. Departures only between 6am and 8:30am and on condition the bus is full. Reckon on 80 yuan.

▶ *By local transport*

Local buses are much cheaper (25 yuan), but take 4 hours to reach the site after a tedious journey. Buses leave Beijing from Majuan (马圈) coach station, and stop at Zunhua (遵化), where you take a minibus for the Qing Tombs. If you are planning on doing the trip in a day, leave early in the morning.

▶ *By taxi*

Quicker, but more expensive. Moreover make sure the driver knows the way well: few tourists visit the Qing Tombs. Reckon on 400 yuan to go there and back in a day from Beijing, divided by the number of passengers in the car.

▶ *On site*

The basic points of the Qing Tombs can be visited on foot. Reckon on 2 to 3 hours. If you are pushed for time, motorcycles can take you from one tomb to another: take time to negotiate a deal before setting off.

Where to stay

There is little in the way of accommodation on site, unless you can sort something out with the occupant. A hotel is open south of the car park.

▶ *Qingfeng Hotel*

清风宾馆

Tel (0315) 6949216/65 rooms

From the car park go for 500 metres as far as the sign marking the hotel on the right. Double rooms are a bit overpriced (160 yuan), but some triples are more worthwhile (150 yuan). It's all pretty basic, but fairly clean and practical. Better to arrange some food in advance. In high season, you'll find some stalls around the car park at the entrance to the site.

Eastern Royal Tombs of the Qing Dynasty

清东陵

8am-4:30pm, in summer 5:30pm/120 yuan

The vaults are gathered together in a valley, northeast of Beijing. Five emperors, 14 empresses and more than 130 concubines were buried there, as well as several high ranking people close to the imperial family. The Qing emperor Qianlong, who reigned from 1735 to 1795, was buried on this site. His tomb, or rather what tomb raiders have left standing, is one of the most impressive funeral vaults in China

Qianlong's Tomb (Yuling Tomb)

乾隆墓（裕陵）

The tomb of Emperor Qianlong was the first to be built in the valley. Arranged in the basement of a wooden pavilion, it is sheltered by a massive marble door which was forced open by tomb raiders. The frescos on the door, ceilings and walls of the funereal hall are beautifully decorated with Buddhist sculptures and Sanskrit and Tibetan sutras. The tomb covers an area of 500 square metres.

Cixi's Tomb (Dingdongling Tomb)

慈禧墓（定东陵）

The decorations on the tomb of Empress Dowager Cixi, which can be found in the basement of a palace, are of a slightly lesser quality than those of Qianlong's tomb, but the palace itself is amazingly beautiful. The phoenix, symbol of the empress, and the dragon, symbol of the emperor, are very refined. Like Qianlong's tomb, Cixi's was the target of tomb raiders at the start of the 20th century.

Other tombs

The other tombs are not as well made as the funeral vaults of Qianlong and Cixi, but the walk is worth the effort for the beautiful architecture of the different palaces and the countryside in the valley. Huiling Tomb of Emperor Tongzhi (1856—1874) is the only one closed all year round. All the others are open in season, but many remain closed out of season. An exhibition (5 yuan extra) presents several models of bodies in plaster and a short history.

NOTES

NOTES

NOTES

NOTES

NOTES

NOTES

NOTES

INDEX

A

Accommodation ····················· 19

Acrobats ······························90

Aeroflot ······························47

Air Canada ····························48

Air China······························47

Air France ···························48

Airport Shuttle Bus ···············46

Altar of God of Agriculture ··· 169

At Café ···························· 105

Apartments to rent ···············70

Aperitivo ·····························84

Argentine Tango ···················87

Art Galleries ······················ 104

Assaggi································80

B

Badaling ·························· 201

Bai Feng Bar·························83

Bamboo Garden Hotel ···········70

Banana ·······························87

Bank ···························· 7, 62

Bank of China ······················62

Baoguo Temple··················· 173

Bar Blu ······························84

Bed ··································84

Beihai Park························· 142

Beijing Antique City ··············93

Beijing Art Museum············· 180

Beijing Capital Airport ···········46

Beijing Dadong Roast Duck
    Restaurant ·······················79

Beijing Downtown Backpackers
    Accommodation ·················67

Beijing First Auto Rental ·········60

Beijing Gong ·······················81

Beijing Hotel ·······················66

Beijing International Post and
    Telecommunications Office··· 10

Beijing Lama Temple Youth Hostel
··72

Beijing Miaoshou Foot Massage
··89

Beijing Milun School of Traditional
    Kung Fu ····························88

Beijing Municipal Public Security
    Bureau·······························3

Beijing Museum of Ancient
    Architecture ···················· 169

Beijing Olympics ···················56

Beijing Photographic Equipment
    City ································ 100

Beijing Planning Exhibition Hall
·· 128

Beijing Silk Store ················ 101

Beijing Tokyo Art Projects···· 105

Beijing Tourism Information Centre
··· 16

Beijing Tourist Information Centre
··· 61

Bell Tower ························· 142

Bellagio ·······························79

Bicycle Kingdom ···················60

Bicycle Rental·······················60

Bird market···························91

Biyong Hall························· 161

Bodhi·······························88

British Airways ····················48

British Council China Beijing···99

Buddha of Longevity ··········· 159

C

Café de la Poste···················81

Café Sambal························77

Caldron Street··················· 157

Caochangdi ······················ 105

Capital Museum ················· 179

Capital Theatre···················91

China Puppet Theatre···········90

Chajiafu Tea House ··············83

Chang'an Grand Theatre········90

Changling Tomb ················· 209

Chaoyang District ·············· 150

Chaoyang Theatre················90

Cherry Lane Movies··············88

China Buddhism College ······ 170

China Eastern ·····················47

China Millenium Monument Art
  Museum··························· 102

China National Tourism
  Administration ··················· 16

China World Hotel ················72

China World Trade Centre ······98

Chinese Contemporary Beijing
  ···································· 105

Chinese food ······················22

Chinese manners ················· 17

Chinese postal service ··········33

Chongwen District··············· 163

Cigarettes ···························7

Cinema ·····························88

City Hotel···························72

Cixi's Tomb························ 213

Climbing at Boulder Bar·········87

Clothes ······························6

Coal Hill Park····················· 138

Commune by the Great Wall—
  Kempinski Hotels ············· 199

Confucius Institute Headquarters
  ···································· 102

Confucius Temple················ 159

Courtyard Gallery ··············· 104

Credit cards ························6

Cuimingzhuang Hotel ············66

Cultural life ·······················26

Currency·····························5

D

Dadu ······························ 107

Daguanlou ·························88

Dashanzi 798 Art Factory····· 104

Daxin Textile Store·············· 101

Dashilan ···························95

Dingdongling Tomb ············· 213

Dingling Tomb ···················· 210

Disabled travelers··················7

Ditan Park·························· 162

Don't dos ··························· 18

Dongdan Indoor Swimming Pool
  ·····································87

Dongzhimen Coach Station ····49

Dragon Air ·························47

Dragonfly···························89

Drinks ·····························25

Driving licence ⋯⋯⋯⋯⋯⋯⋯4

Drum Tower ⋯⋯⋯⋯⋯⋯⋯ 140

E

Eastern Royal Tombs of the Qing Dynasty ⋯⋯⋯⋯⋯⋯⋯⋯ 213

Eatea Tea House ⋯⋯⋯⋯⋯⋯82

Echo Wall ⋯⋯⋯⋯⋯⋯⋯ 168

Electricity ⋯⋯⋯⋯⋯⋯⋯⋯8

Embassies in Beijing ⋯⋯⋯⋯8

Emperor Chengzu ⋯⋯⋯⋯ 209

Emperor Qianlong ⋯⋯⋯⋯ 213

Emperor Tongzhi ⋯⋯⋯⋯ 213

emperor's throne ⋯⋯⋯⋯ 132

Empress Dowager Cixi ⋯⋯ 213

EMS ⋯⋯⋯⋯⋯⋯⋯⋯⋯ 10

Etiquette ⋯⋯⋯⋯⋯⋯⋯ 16

Exchang ⋯⋯⋯⋯⋯⋯5, 7, 62

F

Fangshan Restaurant ⋯⋯⋯ 74

Far East Hotel ⋯⋯⋯⋯⋯ 73

Far East International Youth Hostel ⋯⋯⋯⋯⋯⋯⋯⋯ 73

Festivals ⋯⋯⋯⋯⋯⋯⋯ 29

Five-Pagoda Temple ⋯⋯⋯ 183

FLTRP ⋯⋯⋯⋯⋯⋯⋯⋯ 11

Forbidden City ⋯⋯⋯⋯⋯ 129

forest of steles ⋯⋯⋯⋯⋯ 183

Fragrant Hills Park ⋯⋯⋯⋯ 193

French Cultural Centre ⋯⋯ 100

Friendship Store ⋯⋯⋯⋯⋯95

G

Gaobeidian ⋯⋯⋯⋯⋯⋯⋯98

Garden of Harmonious Virtue ⋯⋯⋯⋯⋯⋯⋯⋯⋯ 191

Gate of Divine Prowess ⋯⋯ 135

Gate of Heavenly Purity ⋯⋯ 134

Gate of Supreme Harmony⋯ 130

Genghis Khan ⋯⋯⋯⋯⋯ 107

Get Lucky Bar ⋯⋯⋯⋯⋯⋯85

Ghost Street ⋯⋯⋯⋯⋯⋯ 157

Gold lions ⋯⋯⋯⋯⋯⋯⋯ 132

Golden Water ⋯⋯⋯⋯⋯⋯ 130

Golden Weeks ⋯⋯⋯⋯⋯⋯2

Green Tea House ⋯⋯⋯⋯⋯80

Guesthouses ⋯⋯⋯⋯⋯⋯ 19

Gui Jie ⋯⋯⋯⋯⋯⋯⋯⋯80

Guided tours of Beijing ⋯⋯87

Guo Moruo ⋯⋯⋯⋯⋯⋯ 144

Guo Moruo's Former Residence ⋯⋯⋯⋯⋯⋯⋯⋯ 144

H

Haidian District ⋯⋯⋯⋯⋯ 175

Hailong Shopping Mall ⋯⋯ 100

Hall of Benevolence and Longevity ⋯⋯⋯⋯⋯⋯⋯⋯ 191

Hall of Celestial Kings ⋯⋯ 170

Hall of Great Accomplishments ⋯⋯⋯⋯⋯⋯⋯⋯ 160

Hall of Middle Harmony ⋯⋯ 134

Hall of Prayer for Good Harvest ⋯⋯⋯⋯⋯⋯⋯⋯ 168

Hall of Preserving Harmony 134

Hall of Religious Law 174

Hall of Saint Worship 187

Hall of Supreme Harmony 132

Hall of Union........................ 134

Handicraft 99

Hao Yuan Hotel 64

Hatsune 79

Health 4

Hejinghfu Hotel......................68

Here 83

Hertz....................................60

Holidays 9

Hongqiao Market...................95

Hospitals...............................63

Hotel Kapok 65

Hotels...................................20

HSBC....................................62

Hua Jia Yi Yuan 80

Huairou District 197

Huanghuacheng.................. 203

Huatong International Youth
    Hostel 71

Huiling Tomb 213

Human Race Gallery............ 166

Imperial College 161

Imperial Garden 135

Imperial Peace Hall 135

Imperial Vault of Heaven 168

Incense Burner Peak 193

Inner Affairs..........................87

Internet 10, 62

Jade Disc Hall 161

Jade Emperor's Hall 174

Jade International Youth Hostel
   64

Jade Islet 142

jade urn 143

Jiao Lou Business Hotel 64

Jicheng 107

Jin Dynasty 106

Jingfu Pavilion 192

Jinshan Hotel...................... 199

Jinshanling 205

Jintang Villa 198

Juyongguan Pass 201

Kao Rou Ji 76

Ke Jia Cai 76

KLM Royal Dutch Airlines 48

Kong Yiji 77

Kublai Khan......................... 107

Kunming Lake...................... 191

Lan 85

Lao She 146

Lao She Tea House................89

Lao She's Former Residence

.... 146

Leo Hostel 73

Li Family Imperial Cuisine 78

Liao Dynasty 107

Liqun Roast Duck Restaurant
.... 81

Liulichang 97

Liuliqiao Coach Station 49

Local time 2

Long Corridor 191

Longevity Hill 191

Lu Xun 184

Lu Xun Museum 183

Lufthansa Airlines 48

Lu Song Yuan Hotel 69

M

Made in China 75

Mail 10

Making gifts locally 6

Mao Dun 148

Mao Dun's Former Residence
.... 148

Mao Zedong 127

Marble Boat 192

Marble ramp 134

Marco Polo 107

Markets 92

Martial arts 90

Massage 88

Media 10

Mei Fu 78

Mei Lanfang 144

Mei Lanfang's Former Residence

.... 143

Memorial Hall of Chairman Mao
.... 123

Menu 21

Meridian Gate 130

Military Museum 175

Millennium Monument 178

Ming City Wall Ruins Park 152

Ming Dynasty 107

Ming Tombs 207

Mix 86

Miyun County 197

Monument to the People's Heroes
.... 124

Mount Shou'an 193

Museums 102

Museums of History and of the
Revolution 124

Music Bars 85

Muslim 171

Must dos 17

Mutianyu 202

N

Nali Mall 99

Nameless Highland 86

Nanjing 107

National Art Museum of China
.... 102

National Museum of China 124

National Theatre 91

Natural History Museum 166

New China 107

Night life 27

Noble Restaurant ·················· 77

North Lake ························· 142

Novotel Peace····················· 66

Nuage································ 77

Nüren Jie Flower Market ········ 95

O

Old Beijing Observatory ······ 153

Old Legations Quarter (in Beijing)
································· 163

Olympic Sports Venues (in Beijing)
·································· 58

Opening times ····················· 13

Outdoor equipment store······· 99

Ox Street Mosque ·············· 170

P

Palace of Earthly Tranquillity
·································· 135

Palace of Heavenly Purity····· 134

Palace of Prince Gong ·········· 144

Panjiayuan Antiques Market ···92

Pass By Bar····················· 76

Pavilion of Ten Thousand
    Happinesses ·················· 157

Peking Man ····················· 106

Peking Opera ······················ 89

Peking Union Medical College
    Hospital ·························4

Peninsula Palace ·················· 67

People's Art Experimental Theatre
·································· 91

Photography··················13, 100

Ping An Fu Hotel ··················· 69

Poachers Inn ······················ 86

Post office························· 62

Pre-paid travel cards ············· 60

Press ···························· 11

Pure Lotus Vegetarian ··········· 80

Purple Bamboo Park············ 180

Q

Qianlong's Tomb ················· 213

Qianmen Dajie···················· 139

Qianmen Gate ···················· 121

Qing Dynasty ····················· 107

Qing Tombs ······················· 211

Qingfeng Hotel ··················· 212

Qomolangma Hotel ··············· 69

Quanjude ··························· 82

R

Red Capital Residence ··········· 70

Red Gate Gallery················· 104

Red House ························· 71

Ritan Office Building············· 98

Ritan Park··························· 155

Rock'N'Roll························· 86

Round Altar······················· 167

Round City ························· 143

Rulai Hall ························· 153

S

Saga Youth Hostel················ 64

Sanlitun ·························· 151

Scared Way ························· 209

Sea of Wisdom Temple ········ 192

Senior travellers ····················7

798 Space···························· 10

17-Arch Bridage·················· 191

Shanghai Air························· 47

Shopping ···························· 30

Shows ························· 26, 89

Shun Yi Fu·························· 74

Sihe Hotel ·························· 65

Silk Market························· 94

Sima Restaurant & Hotel······ 198

Simatai ····························· 204

Sleeping Buddha Temple······ 193

Song Qingling ···················· 146

Song Qingling's Former Residence
··································· 146

Source of Law Temple ········ 170

Southeast Tower················ 153

South Silk Road ·················· 76

Spin ······························· 99

Sporting and activities····· 26, 87

St Regis ···························· 72

Statue of Buddha ·············· 153

Statue of Confucius············· 159

stone tablets ····················· 159

Summer Palace··················· 189

Sun Yat-sen······················· 127

Suzie Wong ························ 86

T

Tango ······························ 86

Telephone ···················· 14, 62

Temple of Ancient Monarchs
··································· 187

Temple of Great Charity······· 188

Temple of Heaven ·············· 167

Temple of Heavenly Peace···· 173

Temple of Longevity ··········· 180

Temple of the Azure Clouds ··· 193

Temple of the Earth Park ····· 162

Temple of the Eastern Peak ··· 156

Temple of the Sun Park········ 155

Temple of Wisdom Attained ··· 153

The Courtyard ···················· 75

The Drum & Bell ·················· 83

The Great Hall of the People
··································· 126

The Great wall ··················· 201

The International Post Office
··································· 62

The Le Quai························· 79

The Red Theatre ·················· 90

The Regent Beijing··············· 67

The Source························· 78

The 13 Sutra Table Forest···· 160

Theatre and dance ··············· 91

Thinking Hands··················· 105

Three Guizhou Men ·············· 79

Tian Fu ···························· 101

Tian'anmen Rostrum ··········· 127

Tian'anmen Square ············· 121

Tiandi Yijia ························· 75

Tianqiao Acrobatics ·············· 91

Timezone 8 ······················ 105

Tourist Hotline ···················· 61

Tourism offices ··············16, 61

Tower of Buddhist Incense ··· 191

Traditional toys ·················· 101

Travellers cheques ················ 5

Travelling with children ··········· 6

22 Film café ························· 84

U

Underground City ·············· 170

Units of length ···················· 16

Useful numbers ·················· 15

V

Vaccinations ························· 3

Vics ································· 87

Visa ································· 3

W

Waiting for Godot ················ 83

Wanfu Pavilion ·················· 157

Wangfujing Dajie ··········· 98, 139

Wangfujing Foreign Languages
Bookstore ························ 99

Wangfujing Xiaochi Jie ··········· 74

Weather ··························· 16

West Station ······················ 49

What? Bar ·························· 86

White Cloud Temple ··········· 173

White Dagoba ···················· 143

White Dagoba Temple ·········· 185

Working People's Cultural Palace
································· 128

X

Xiangshenghang ················· 100

Xiaohong's Hostel ·············· 198

Xicheng District ················· 175

Xindong Cheng Gallery ········ 105

Xin Dong'an Cinema ············· 88

Xuanwu District ················· 163

Y

Yanjing ··························· 107

Yansui Pavilion ··················· 159

Yaxiu Market ······················ 94

Yong'an Temple ················· 142

Yonghegong Lama Temple ··· 157

Youhao Guesthouse ············· 68

Youth hostels ····················· 19

Youyi Youth Hostel ··············· 71

Youzhou ·························· 107

Yuan Dynasty ···················· 107

Yuanmingyuan ··················· 192

Yugongyishan ····················· 85

Yuling Tomb ······················ 213

Yuyuantan Park ·················· 180

Z

Zhang Qun Jia ····················· 78

Zhaogongkou Coach Station ··· 49

Zhaoling Tomb ··················· 210

Zhaolong Youth Hostel ··········· 71

Zhongdu ·························· 107

Zhonghai Computer Market ·· 100

Zhongshan Park ················· 127

Zhou Dynasty ···················· 106

Zhu Di ··························· 107

Zhu Yijun ························· 210

Map I ·························· 110, 111

Map II ······························ 114

Map III ························ 112, 113

Map IV······························· 109

Subway································ 115

Place Museum ···················· 131